백성을 가르치는 바른 소리 글자

훈민정음

세종 외 8인 지음

김슬옹 편역

훈민정음 해례본
현대말·영문 손바닥책을
펴내며

579돌 한글날, KBS는 〈흥해라! 나랏말씀〉(연출 이광록)이라는 특집 방송을 내보냈습니다. 방송의 모든 순간이 감동적이었지만, 특히 외국인을 포함한 다양한 출연자들이 '훈민정음 해례본'(이하 해례본)을 함께 낭독하는 장면이 깊은 인상을 남겼습니다.

해례본은 온 국민이, 아니 전 세계인이 함께 읽어야 할 고전 중의 고전입니다. 호주머니에 넣고 다니며 언제 어디서든 꺼내 읽을 수 있는 손바닥책으로 펴낸 까닭이 바로 여기에 있습니다. 세종대왕께서 창제·반포한 훈민정음의 가치를 국내외 독자들과 공유하고자 하는 바람으로 한국어판과 영어판을 함께 엮었습니다.

　세종대왕이 훈민정음을 반포한 뜻은 분명했습니다. 누구나 쉬운 문자로 느낌과 생각을 마음껏 표현하고 나누어야 한다는 것이었습니다. 이 작은 책이 국내외 독자 여러분께 훈민정음의 보편적 창제 정신을 나누고, 이 문자가 참다운 지혜의 세상을 어떻게 열게 되었는지 함께 공감하는 계기가 되기를 바랍니다.

　쉽고 정확한 영어 번역을 해주신 조던 드웨거 선생님과 영어 번역을 꼼꼼히 살펴주신 정필정 선생님께 깊이 감사드립니다.

2025년 한글날에 김슬옹

1부
정음(바른소리 글자)

우리나라 말이 중국말과 달라 한자와는 서로 잘 통하지 않는다. 그러므로 글 모르는 백성이 말하려는 것이 있어도, 끝내 제 뜻을 능히 펼치지 못하는 사람이 많다. 내가 이것을 가엾게 여겨 새로 스물여덟 자를 만드니, 사람마다 쉽게 익혀 날마다 씀에 편안케 하고자 할 따름이다.

ㄱ[기]는 어금닛소리(아음)이니 '군(君)'자의 처음 나는 소리(초성)와 같다. 나란히 쓰면 '끃(虯)'자의 처음 나는 소리와 같다. ㅋ[키]는 어금닛소리이니, '쾌(快)'자의 처음 나는 소리와 같다.

ㆁ[이]는 어금닛소리이니, '업(業)'자의 처음 나는 소리와 같다.

ㄷ[디]는 혓소리(설음)이니, '둫(斗)'자의 처음 나는 소리와 같다. 나란히 쓰면 '땀(覃)'자의 처음 나는 소리와 같다. ㅌ[티]는 혓소리이니, '톤(呑)'자의 처음 나는 소리와 같다. ㄴ[니]는 혓소리이니, '나(那)'자의 처음 나는 소리와 같다.

ㅂ[비]는 입술소리(순음)이니, '볃(彆)'자의 처음 나는 소리와 같다. 나란히 쓰면 '뽀(步)'자의 처음 나는 소리와 같다. ㅍ[피]는 입술소리이니, '표(漂)'자의 처음 나는 소리와 같다. ㅁ[미]는 입술소리이니, '미(彌)'자의 처음 나는 소리와 같다.

ㅈ[지]는 잇소리(치음)이니, '즉(即)'자의 처음 나는 소리와 같다. 나란히 쓰면 'ㅉ(慈)'자의 처음 나는 소리와 같다. ㅊ[치]는 잇소리이니, '침(侵)'자의 처음 나는 소리와 같다. ㅅ[시]는 잇소리이니, '슌(戍)'자의 처음 나는 소리와 같다. 나란히 쓰면 'ㅆ(邪)'자의 처음 나는 소리와 같다.

ㆆ[히]는 목구멍소리(후음)이니, '흡(挹)'자의 처음 나는 소리와 같다. ㅎ[히]는 목구멍소리이니, '허(虛)'자의 처음 나는 소리와 같다. 나란히 쓰면 'ㆅ(洪)'자의 처음 나는 소리와 같다. ㅇ[이]는 목구멍소리이니, '욕(欲)'자의 처음 나는 소리와 같다.

ㄹ[리]는 반혓소리(반설음)이니, '려(閭)'자의 처음 나는 소리와 같다. ㅿ[싀]는 반잇소리(반치음)이니, '샹(穰)'자의 처음 나는 소리와 같다.

ㆍ는 '퉅(呑)'자의 가운뎃소리(중성)와 같다. ㅡ는 '즉(即)'자의 가운뎃소리와 같다. ㅣ는 '침(侵)'자의 가

운뎃소리와 같다.

ㅗ는 '홍(洪)'자의 가운뎃소리와 같다. ㅏ는 '땀(覃)'자의 가운뎃소리와 같다. ㅜ는 '군(君)'자의 가운뎃소리와 같다. ㅓ는 '업(業)'자의 가운뎃소리와 같다.

ㅛ는 '욕(欲)'자의 가운뎃소리와 같다. ㅑ는 '샹(穰)'자의 가운뎃소리와 같다. ㅠ는 '슏(戌)'자의 가운뎃소리와 같다. ㅕ는 '볃(彆)'자의 가운뎃소리와 같다.

끝소리글자(종성자)는 첫소리글자(초성자)를 다시 쓴다.

ㅇ[이]를 입술소리글자 아래 이어 쓰면 곧 입술가벼운소리글자(순경음자, ㅸ)가 된다. 첫소리글자(초성자)를 합쳐서 쓰려면 나란히 쓰고, 끝소리글자(종성자)도 첫소리글자(초성자)와 마찬가지다. ㆍ ㅡ ㅗ ㅜ ㅛ ㅠ는 첫소리글자 아래에 붙여 쓴다. ㅣ ㅏ ㅓ ㅑ ㅕ는 첫소리글자의 오른쪽에 붙여 쓴다. 무릇 낱글자는 반드시 합하여야만 음절이 이루어진다.

음절자 왼쪽에 한 점을 더하면 거성(높은 소리)이고, 점이 둘이면 상성(처음이 낮고 나중이 높은 소리)이고, 점이 없으면 평성(낮은 소리)이다. 입성(짧고 빨리 끝나는 소리)은 점을 더하는 것은 평성·상성·거성과 같으나 빠르다.

2부
정음해례(바른소리 글자 풀이)

1. 제자해(글자 만든 풀이)

하늘과 땅 사이에 변하지 않는 이치는 오직 음양오행 하나뿐이다. 곤괘(여성다움이 가장 센 상징, ☷)와 복괘(싹이 트는 상징, ☳)의 사이가 태극이 되고, 움직임과 멈춤 작용으로 음양이 된다. 무릇 하늘과 땅 사이에 살아 있는 것들이 음양을 버리고 어디로 가겠는가? 그러므로 사람의 말소리(성음) 모두 음양의 이치가 있는 것인데, 생각해 보니 사람들이 살피지 못했을 뿐이다.

이제 정음이 만들어지게 된 것도 애초부터 지혜를 굴리고 힘들여 찾은 것이 아니고, 단지 말소리의 이치를 끝까지 파고들었을 뿐이다. 그 이치가 이미 둘이 아니니, 어찌 천지자연의 혼령과 신령스러운 정령과 함께 정음을 쓰지 않겠는가?

정음 스물여덟 자는 각각 그 모양을 본떠서 만들었다. 첫소리글자는 모두 열일곱 자다. 어금닛소리글자 ㄱ[기]는 혀뿌리가 목구멍을 막는 모양을 본떴다. 혓소리글자 ㄴ[니]는 혀가 윗잇몸에 닿는 모양을 본떴다. 입술소리글자 ㅁ[미]는 입 모양을 본떴다. 잇소리글자 ㅅ[시]는 이 모양을 본떴다. 목구멍소리글자 ㅇ[이]는 목구멍 모양을 본떴다.

ㅋ[키]는 ㄱ[기]에 비해서 소리가 조금 세게 나는

까닭으로 획을 더하였다. ㄴ[니]에서 ㄷ[디], ㄷ[디]에서 ㅌ[티], ㅁ[미]에서 ㅂ[비], ㅂ[비]에서 ㅍ[피], ㅅ[시]에서 ㅈ[지], ㅈ[지]에서 ㅊ[치], ㅇ[이]에서 ㆆ[히], ㆆ[히]에서 ㅎ[히]가 됨도 그 소리로 말미암아 획을 더한 뜻은 같으나, 다만 ㆁ[이]만은 다르다. 반혓소리글자 ㄹ[리], 반잇소리글자 ㅿ[싀]도 또한 혀와 이의 모양을 본떴으나, 그 짜임새를 달리해서 만들었기에 획을 더한 뜻은 없다.

무릇 사람의 말소리는 오행에 뿌리를 두고 있다. 그러므로 사계절에 합하여도 어그러짐이 없으며, 오음계와 맞추어 봐도 잘 어울리고 틀리지 않는다.

목구멍은 깊숙하고 젖어 있으니 오행으로는 물이다. 말소리가 비어 있는 듯이 통하므로 이는 물이 투명하게 맑아 잘 흐르는 것과 같다. 계절로는 겨울이고, 음률로는 '우음계'다.

'어금니'는 어긋나고 기니 오행으로는 나무다. 어

금닛소리는 목구멍소리와 비슷하나 목이 꽉 차므로 나무가 물에서 나되 형체가 있는 것과 같다. 계절로는 봄이고, 음률로는 '각음계'다.

혀는 재빠르게 움직이니 오행으로는 불이다. 혓소리가 구르고 날리는 것은 불이 타올라 퍼지며 위아래로 오르내림과 같다. 계절로는 여름이고, 음률로는 '치음계'다.

이는 억세고 끊을 듯 날카로우니 오행으로는 쇠다. 잇소리가 가루처럼 부서지고 걸리는 듯하게 나는 것은 쇠가 부스러졌다가 다시 불에 달구어 두드리면 단단해지는 것과 같다. 계절로는 가을이고, 음률로는 '상음계'다.

입술은 모난 것이 나란히 합해지니, 오행으로는 땅이다. 입술소리가 머금으며 넓은 것은 땅이 만물을 머금으니 넓고 큰 것과 같다. 계절로는 늦여름이고, 음률로는 '궁음계'다.

물은 만물을 낳는 근원이요, 불은 만물을 이루어지게 하는 작용이므로 오행 가운데서 물·불이 으뜸이다. 목구멍은 소리가 나오는 문이요, 혀는 소리를 가려내는 악기이므로 오음 가운데서 목구멍소리와 혓소리가 으뜸이 된다.

목구멍은 안쪽에 있고 어금니는 그 앞에 있으므로 북쪽과 동쪽의 방위다. 혀와 이가 또한 그다음에 있으니 남쪽과 서쪽의 방위다. 입술은 끝에 있으니, 오행의 흙이 일정한 방위가 없이 네 계절에 기대어 네 계절을 왕성하게 함을 뜻한다. 이런즉 첫소리 속에도 자체의 음양오행과 방위의 수가 있는 것이다.

또 말소리를 '맑음과 흐림(청탁)'으로 말해 보자. ㄱㄷㅂㅈㅅㆆ[기디비지시히]는 아주 맑은소리 '전청'이 된다. ㅋㅌㅍㅊㅎ[키티피치히]는 덜 맑은소리 '차청'이 된다. ㄲㄸㅃㅉㅆㆅ[끼띠삐찌씨혜]는 아주 흐린소리 '전탁'이 된다. ㆁㄴㅁㅇㄹㅿ[이니미이리시]

는 맑지도 흐리지도 않은 '불청불탁(울림소리)'이 된다.

　ㄴㅁㅇ[니미이]는 소리가 가장 세지 않으므로, 차례로는 비록 뒤에 있으나, 모양을 본떠 글자를 만드는 시초가 된다. ㅅ[시]와 ㅈ[지]는 비록 다 아주 맑은 소리 '전청'이지만 ㅅ[시]는 ㅈ[지]에 비하여 소리가 거세지 않으므로 글자를 만드는 데 시초가 되었다. 오직 어금닛소리의 ㆁ[이]는 비록 혀뿌리가 목구멍을 막아서 코로 소리 기운이 나가지만 ㆁ[이]의 소리는 ㅇ[이]와 비슷해서 중국 한자음 사전(운서)에서도 ㆁ[이]와 ㅇ[이]가 많이 혼용되니, 이제 ㆁ[이]는 목구멍을 본떠 만들었으되, 어금닛소리글자를 만드는 시초로 삼지 않았다. 대개 목구멍은 물에 속하고 어금니는 나무에 속하는 까닭에 ㆁ[이]는 비록 어금니에 속해 있으면서도 ㅇ[이]와 비슷하여 마치 나무의 싹이 물에서 나와 부드러우며 오히려 물기가 많은 것과 같기 때문이다.

ㄱ[기]는 나무가 바탕을 이룬 것이고, ㅋ[키]는 나무가 무성하게 자란 것이고, ㄲ[끼]는 나무가 오래되어 굳건해진 것이니, 이는 한결같이 모두 어금니를 본뜬 데서 비롯된 것이다.

아주 맑은소리 '전청' 글자를 나란히 쓰면 아주 흐린소리 '전탁'이 되는 것은 아주 맑은 소리가 엉기면 아주 흐린소리가 되기 때문이다. 다만, 목구멍소리만은 덜 맑은소리 '차청'이 아주 흐린소리 '전탁'이 되는데, 그것은 대개 ㆆ[히]는 소리가 깊어서 엉기지 않고, ㅎ[히]는 ㆆ[히]에 비하여 소리가 얕아서 엉기어 아주 흐린소리 '전탁'이 되기 때문이다.

ㅇ[이]를 입술소리글자 아래에 이어 쓰면 곧 입술가벼운소리글자(순경음자)가 되는데, 이러한 입술가벼운 소리는 입술이 살짝 다물어지면서 목구멍소리가 많아지기 때문이다.

가운뎃소리글자는 모두 열한 자다. ㆍ는 혀가 오

그라드니 소리가 깊어서, 하늘이 자시(밤 11시~오전 1시)에서 열리는 것과 같다. 둥근 글꼴은 하늘을 본떴다. ㅡ는 혀가 조금 오그라드니 소리가 깊지도 얕지도 않으므로 땅이 축시(오전 1시~3시)에서 열리는 것과 같다. 평평한 글꼴은 땅을 본떴다. ㅣ는 혀가 오그라지지 않아 소리는 얕으니, 사람이 인시(오전 3시~5시)에서 생기는 것과 같다. 바로 선 글꼴은 사람을 본떴다.

다음 여덟 가운뎃소리는 어떤 것은 입을 오므려서 어떤 것은 입을 벌려서 발음한다.

ㅗ는 ·와 같은 가운뎃소리(양성모음)나 입을 더 오므리며, 그 모양이 ·가 ㅡ와 합해서 이루어진 것은 하늘과 땅이 처음으로 사귄다는 뜻을 담았다. ㅏ는 ·와 같은 가운뎃소리(양성모음)이나 입을 더 벌리며 그 모양은 ㅣ와 ·가 서로 합하여 이루어진 것으로, 하늘과 땅의 쓰임이 일과 사물에서 나타나 사

람을 기다려 이루어진다는 뜻을 담은 것이다.

ㅜ는 ㅡ와 같은 가운뎃소리(음성모음)이나 입을 더 오므리며, 그 모양이 ㅡ가 ·와 합해서 이루어진 것은 역시 하늘과 땅이 처음으로 사귄다는 뜻을 담았다. ㅓ는 ㅡ와 같은 가운뎃소리(음성모음)이나 입을 더 벌리니, 그 모양은 ·와 ㅣ가 합해서 이루어진 것이며, 역시 하늘과 땅의 쓰임이 일과 사물에서 나타나되 사람을 기다려서 이루어진 뜻을 담은 것이다.

ㅛ는 ㅗ와 같은 가운뎃소리(양성모음)이나, 그 소리는 ㅣ에서 비롯된다. ㅑ는 ㅏ와 같은 가운뎃소리(양성모음)이나, 그 소리는 ㅣ에서 비롯된다. ㅠ는 ㅜ와 같은 가운뎃소리(음성모음)이나, 그 소리는 ㅣ에서 비롯된다. ㅕ는 ㅓ와 같은 가운뎃소리(음성모음)이나, 그 소리는 ㅣ에서 비롯된다.

ㅗㅏㅜㅓ는 하늘과 땅에서 비롯된 것이므로 '처음 나온 것(초출자)'이다. ㅛㅑㅠㅕ는 ㅣ에서 비롯되

어 사람(ㅣ)을 겸하였으므로 '거듭 나온 것(재출자)'이다. ㅗㅏㅜㅓ에서 둥근 것(•)을 하나로 한 것은 '처음 생긴 것(초생자)'이라는 뜻을 담았다. ㅛㅑㅠㅕ에서 그 둥근 것(•)을 둘로 한 것은 '다시 생겨난 것(재생자)'이라는 뜻을 담은 것이다.

ㅗㅏㅛㅑ의 둥근 것(•)이 위와 밖에 놓인 것은 하늘(•)에서 나와 양성이 되기 때문이다. ㅜㅓㅠㅕ의 둥근 것(•)이 아래쪽과 안쪽에 있는 것은 땅(ㅡ)에서 나와 음성이 되기 때문이다.

•가 여덟 가운뎃소리글자에 두루 다 있는 것은 마치 양성이 음성을 거느리고 만물에 두루 흐름과 같다. ㅛㅑㅠㅕ가 모두 사람을 뜻하는 ㅣ소리가 들어 있는 것은 사람이 만물의 영장으로 능히 하늘(양)과 땅(음)이 하는 일에 참여할 수 있기 때문이다.

가운뎃소리글자들은 하늘(•), 땅(ㅡ), 사람(ㅣ)을 본뜬 것을 가졌으니, 삼재(하늘·땅·사람) 이치가 갖추어졌다. 그러므로 하늘·땅·사람의 삼재가 만물의 우선이 되고, 하늘이 삼재의 시작이 되는 것과 같이 ㆍㅡㅣ석 자가 여덟 가운뎃소리글자의 머리가 되고, 또한 ㆍ자가 석 자의 으뜸이 됨과 같다.

ㅗ가 처음으로 하늘에서 생겨나니 하늘의 수로는 1이고 물을 낳는 자리다. ㅏ가 다음으로 생겨나니 하늘의 수로는 3이고 나무를 낳는 자리다. ㅜ가 처음으로 땅에서 나니 땅의 수로는 2이고 불을 낳는 자리다. ㅓ가 다음으로 생겨난 것이니 땅의 수로는 4이고 쇠를 낳는 자리다.

ㅛ가 두 번째로 하늘에서 생겨나니 하늘의 수로는 7이고 불을 이루는 수다. ㅑ가 다음으로 생겨나니 하늘의 수로는 9이고 쇠를 이루는 수다. ㅠ가 두 번째로 땅에서 생겨나니 땅의 수로는 6이고 물을 이루는 수다. ㅕ가 다음으로 생겨나니 땅의 수로는 8이고 나무를 이루는 수다.

물(ㅗㅠ)과 불(ㅜㅛ)은 아직 기를 벗어나지 못하고 음과 양이 서로 사귀어 어울리는 처음이기 때문에, 그것을 발음할 때는 입을 오므린다. 나무(ㅏㅕ)와 쇠(ㅓㅑ)는 음과 양의 바탕을 바로 고정한 것이기 때문에 입을 벌린다.

·는 하늘의 수로는 5이고 흙을 낳는 자리다. ㅡ는 땅의 수로는 10이고 흙을 이루는 수다. ㅣ만 홀로 자리와 수가 없는 것은 대개 사람은 곧 무극의 참과 음양과 오행의 정기가 묘하게 어울리고 엉기어서, 진실로 자리를 정하고 수를 이루는 것을 밝힐 수 없기 때문이다. 이런즉 가운뎃소리(중성) 속에도 또한 저절로 음양과 오행, 방위의 수가 있는 것이다.

첫소리와 가운뎃소리를 맞대어 말해 보자. 가운뎃소리의 음성과 양성은 하늘의 이치다. 첫소리의 단단함과 부드러움은 땅의 이치다. 가운뎃소리는 어떤 것은 깊고 어떤 것은 얕고, 어떤 것은 오므리고 어떤 것은 벌리니, 이런즉 음양이 나뉘고, 오행의 기운이 갖추어지니 하늘의 작용이다.

첫소리는 어떤 것은 비고(목구멍소리), 어떤 것은 막히고(어금닛소리), 어떤 것은 날리고(혓소리), 어떤 것은 걸리고(잇소리), 어떤 것은 무겁고(입술무거운소리), 어떤 것은 가벼우니(입술가벼운소리), 이런즉 곧 단단하고 부드러운 것이 드러나서 여기에 오행의 바탕이 이루어진 것이니 땅의 공이다.

가운뎃소리가 깊고 얕고 오므라지고 벌림으로써 앞서 부르고, 첫소리가 오음의 맑고 흐림으로써 뒤따라 화답하여, 첫소리가 되고 또한 끝소리가 된다. 또한 만물이 땅에서 처음 생겨나서, 다시 땅으로 돌아가는 것으로 볼 수 있다.

첫소리, 가운뎃소리, 끝소리가 합하여 이루어진 글자를 말하자면, 또한 움직임과 고요함이 서로 뿌리가 되어 음과 양이 서로 바뀌는 뜻이 있다. 움직이는 것은 하늘이요, 고요한 것은 땅이다. 움직임과 고요함을 겸한 것은 사람이다.

대개 오행이 하늘에서는 신(우주)의 운행이며, 땅에서는 바탕을 이루는 것이요, 이것이 사람에서는 어짊·예의·믿음·정의·슬기가 신의 운행이요, 간·염통(심장)·지라(비장)·허파(폐장)·콩팥(신장)이 바탕을 이루는 것이다. 첫소리는 움직여 피어나는 뜻이 있으니, 하늘의 일이다. 끝소리는 정해져 멈추는 뜻이 있으니, 땅의 일이다. 가운뎃소리는 첫소리가 생겨난 것을 이어서, 끝소리가 이루어지게 이어주니 사람의 일이다. 대개 글자 소리의 핵심은 가운뎃소리에 있으니, 첫소리·끝소리와 합하여 음절을 이룬다. 또 오히려 하늘과 땅이 만물을 생겨나게 해도, 그것이 쓸모 있게 돕는 것은 반드시 사람한테 힘입음과 같다.

끝소리글자에 첫소리글자를 다시 쓰는 것은 움직여서 양인 것도 하늘이요, 고요해서 음인 것도 하늘이니, 하늘은 실제로는 음과 양으로 나뉜다 하더라도 모든 것을 다스린다. 하나의 바탕 기운이 두루 흘러 다하지 않고, 사계절 바뀜이 돌고 돌아 끝이 없으니 만물의 거둠에서 다시 만물의 처음이 되듯 겨울은 다시 봄이 되는 것이다. 첫소리글자가 다시 끝소리글자가 되고 끝소리글자가 다시 첫소리글자가 되는 것도 역시 이와 같은 뜻이다.

아! 정음이 만들어져 천지 만물의 이치가 모두 갖추어졌으니, 그 정음이 신묘하다. 이는 틀림없이 하늘이 성왕(세종)의 마음을 일깨워, 세종의 손을 빌려 정음을 만들게 한 것이로구나.

갈무리 시

하늘과 땅의 조화는 본디 하나의 기운이니
음양과 오행이 서로 처음이 되며 끝이 되네.

만물이 하늘과 땅 사이에서 꼴과 소리가 있으나
근본은 둘이 아니니 이치와 수로 통하네.

정음 글자 만들 때 주로 그 꼴을 본뜨니
소리 세기에 따라 획을 더하였네.

소리는 어금니·혀·입술·이·목구멍에서 나니
여기에서 첫소리글자 열일곱이 나왔네.

어금닛소리글자는 혀뿌리가 목구멍을 막는 모양을 취하였는데
오직 ㆁ[이]만은 ㅇ[이]와 비슷하나 담은 뜻이 다르네.

혓소리글자는 혀가 윗잇몸에 닿는 모양을 본뜨고
입술소리글자는 바로 입 꼴을 취하였네.

잇소리글자와 목구멍소리글자는 바로 이와 목구멍의 모양을 본떴으니
이 다섯 자 뜻을 알면 소리 이치는 절로 밝혀지네.

또한 반혓소리글자(ㄹ), 반잇소리글자(ㅿ)가 있는데
본뜬 것은 같은데 짜임새가 다르네.

"ㄴ[니], ㅁ[미], ㅅ[시], ㅇ[이]" 소리는 세지 않으므로
차례는 비록 뒤이나 꼴을 본뜨는 처음이 되네.

이것을 네 계절과 천지 기운에 맞추어 보니
오행과 오음계에 어울리지 않음이 없네.

목구멍소리는 '물'이 되니 '겨울'과 '우음계'요
어금닛소리는 '봄'이며 '나무'이니 그 소리는 '각음계'네.

'치음계'에 '여름'이며 '불'인 것은 혓소리요
잇소리는 곧 '상음계'이며 '가을'이니 또한 '쇠'네.

입술소리는 방위와 수가 본디 정해진 것이 없으니
'흙'이며 '늦여름'이니 '궁음계'가 되네.

말소리는 또한 스스로 맑고 흐림이 있으니
중요한 것은 첫소리 날 때에 자세히 헤아려 살펴야 하네.

아주 맑은소리 '전청'은 "ㄱ[기], ㄷ[디], ㅂ[비]"이며
"ㅈ[지], ㅅ[시], ㆆ[히]"도 또한 아주 맑은소리 '전청'이라네.

"ㅋ[키], ㅌ[티], ㅍ[피], ㅊ[치], ㅎ[히]"와 같은 것은
오음 각 하나씩의 덜 맑은소리 '차청'이 되네.

아주 흐린소리 '전탁'은 "ㄲ[끼], ㄸ[띠], ㅃ[삐]"에다
"ㅉ[찌], ㅆ[씨]"가 있고 또한 "ㆅ[혜]"가 있네.

아주 맑은소리 '전청' 글자를 나란히 쓰면 아주 흐린
소리 '전탁' 글자가 되는데
다만 'ㆅ'[혜]만은 'ㅎ[히]'에서 나와 이것만 같지 않네.

"ㆁ[이], ㄴ[니], ㅁ[미], ㅇ[이]"와 "ㄹ[리], ㅿ[싀]"는
그 소리 맑지도 또 흐리지도 않네.

ㅇ[이]를 입술소리에 이어 쓰면 입술가벼운소리가
되는데
목구멍소리가 많아지면서 입술을 살짝 다물어 주네.

가운뎃소리글자 열한 자 또한 꼴을 본떴는데
섬세한 뜻은 아직 쉽게 볼 수 없네.

・는 하늘을 본떠 소리가 가장 깊으니
그래서 둥근 꼴이 총알 같네.

ㅡ 소리는 깊지도 않고 얕지도 않아
그 평평한 꼴은 땅을 본떴네.

ㅣ는 사람이 선 모습을 본뜬 것으로 그 소리 얕으니
하늘·땅·사람의 세 바탕 이치가 이에 갖추어졌네.

ㅗ는 하늘에서 나와 입을 거의 닫으니
하늘의 둥긂과 땅의 평평함을 아울러 담은 것을 본떴네.

ㅏ도 하늘에서 나와 입이 이미 열려 있으니
일과 사물에서 피어나 사람에서 이루어짐이네.

처음 생겨나는 뜻을 사용하여 둥근 점을 하나로 하였으니
하늘에서 나와 '양'이 되어 위와 밖에 놓이네.

ㅛ, ㅑ는 ㅣ를 겸하여 '거듭 나온 것'이 되니
두 개의 둥근 꼴로 그 뜻을 보이네.

ㅜ와 ㅓ와 ㅠ와 ㅕ는 땅에서 나니
보기를 들면 저절로 알 것을 어찌 꼭 풀이를 해야 하랴.

・글자가 여덟 가운뎃소리글자에 두루 있음은
오직 하늘의 작용이 두루 흘러 다님이네.

네 소리(ㅛㅑㅠㅕ)가 사람(ㅣ)을 겸함도 또한 까닭이 있으니

사람(ㅣ)이 하늘과 땅에 참여하는데 가장 신령하기 때문이네.

또 나아가 첫소리·가운데소리·끝소리의 깊은 이치를 캐어 보면
단단함과 부드러움, 음과 양이 저절로 있네.

가운뎃소리는 하늘의 작용으로서 음양으로 나뉘고
첫소리는 땅의 공로로 단단함과 부드러움을 나타내네.

가운뎃소리가 부르면 첫소리가 응하니
하늘이 땅보다 앞섬은 자연의 이치네.

응하는 것이 첫소리도 되고 또 끝소리도 되니
만물이 땅에서 나와 다시 모두 땅으로 되돌아감이네.

음이 바뀌어 양이 되고 양이 바뀌어 음이 되니
한 번 움직이고 한 번 고요함이 서로 뿌리가 되네.

첫소리는 다시 피어나는 뜻이 있으니
양의 움직임으로 하늘의 임자 되네.

끝소리는 땅에 비유되어 음의 고요함이니
글자 소리가 여기서 그쳐 정해지네.

음절을 이루는 핵심은 가운뎃소리의 쓰임새에 있으니
사람이 능히 하늘과 땅의 마땅함을 도울 수 있기 때문이네.

양의 쓰임은 음에 통하니
극에 이르러 뻗으면 도리어 돌아오게 되네.

첫소리글자와 끝소리글자가 비록 하늘과 땅으로 나뉜다고 하나
끝소리글자에 첫소리글자를 쓰는 뜻을 알 수 있네.

정음 글자는 다만 스물여덟 자이지만
심오하고 복잡한 걸 탐구하여 근본 깊이가 어떠한가를 밝혀낼 수 있네.

뜻은 멀되 말은 가까워 백성을 깨우치기 쉬우니
하늘이 주신 것이지 어찌 일찍이 슬기와 기교로 되었으리오.

2. 초성해(첫소리글자 풀이)

정음의 첫소리는 곧 한자음 사전(운서)에서 한 음절

의 첫소리(성모)다. 말소리가 이에서 비롯되므로 이르기를 '어미(모)'라 한 것이다.

　어금닛소리글자는 'ㄱᅮᆫ'자의 첫소리글자인 ㄱ[기]인데, ㄱ[기]가 ᅮᆫ과 어울려 'ㄱᅮᆫ'이 된다. '쾌'자의 첫소리글자는 ㅋ[키]인데, ㅋ[키]가 ㅙ와 합하여 '쾌'가 된다. '끃'자의 첫소리글자는 ㄲ[끼]인데, ㄲ[끼]가 ㅠ와 합하여 '끃'가 된다. '업'자의 첫소리글자는 ㆁ[이]인데, ㆁ[이]가 ㅓㅂ과 합하여 '업'이 되는 따위와 같다. 혓소리글자의 "ㄷㅌㄸㄴ[디티띠니]", 입술소리글자의 "ㅂㅍㅃㅁ[비피삐미]", 잇소리글자의 "ㅈㅊㅉㅅㅆ[지치찌시씨]", 목구멍소리글자의 "ㆆㅎㆅㅇ[히히쪵이]", 반혓소리·반잇소리글자의 "ㄹㅿ[리싀]"도 모두 이와 같다.

갈무리 시

"ㄱㅋㄲㆁ[기키끼이]"는 어금닛소리글자이고
혓소리글자로는 "ㄷㅌ[디티]"와 "ㄸㄴ[띠니]"가 있네.

"ㅂㅍㅃㅁ[비피삐미]"는 곧 입술소리글자이고
잇소리글자로는 "ㅈㅊㅉㅅㅆ[지치찌시씨]"가 있네.

"ㆆㅎㆅㅇ[히히쎠이]"는 곧 목구멍소리글자이고
ㄹ[리]는 반혓소리글자이고, ㅿ[싀]는 반잇소리글자
이네.

스물세 자가 첫소리글자가 되니
온갖 소리가 모두 다 여기에서 생겨나네.

3. 중성해(가운뎃소리글자 풀이)

가운뎃소리는 음절소리(자운)의 가운데에 있으니 첫소리, 끝소리와 합하여 음절을 이룬다. '튼'자의 가운뎃소리글자는 •인데, •가 ㅌ[티]와 ㄴ[은] 사이에 놓여 '튼'이 된다. '즉'자의 가운뎃소리글자는 ㅡ인데, ㅡ는 ㅈ[지]와 ㄱ[윽] 사이에 놓여 '즉'이 된다. '침'자의 가운뎃소리글자는 ㅣ인데, ㅣ가 ㅊ[치]와 ㅁ[음] 사이에 놓여 '침'이 되는 것과 같다. "홍·땀·군·업·욕·샹·슐·별"에서의 "ㅗ ㅏ ㅜ ㅓ ㅛ ㅑ ㅠ ㅕ"도 모두 이와 같다.

두 글자를 합쳐 쓴 것으로, ㅗ와 ㅏ가 똑같이 •와 같은 양성 가운뎃소리이므로 합하여 ㅘ가 된다. ㅛ와 ㅑ도 ㅣ에서 똑같이 비롯되므로 합하면 ㅒ가 된다. ㅜ와 ㅓ가 똑같이 ㅡ와 같은 음성 가운뎃소리이므로 합하여 ㅝ가 된다. ㅠ와 ㅕ가 또한 똑같이 ㅣ에서 비롯되므로 합하여 ㆌ가 된다. 이런 합용자들은 같은 것에서 나와 같은 부류가 되므로, 서로 합해도 어그러지지 않는다.

한 낱글자로 된 가운뎃소리글자가 ㅣ와 서로 합한 것이 열이니 "ㅓ ㅢ ㅚ ㅐ ㅟ ㅔ ㅢ ㅒ ㆌ ㅖ"가 그것이다. 두 낱글자로 된 가운뎃소리글자가 ㅣ와 서로 합한 것은 넷이니 "ㅙ ㅞ ㅙ ㅞ"가 그것이다. ㅣ가 깊고, 얕고, 오므리고, 벌리는 소리에 두루 능히 서로 따를 수 있는 것은 'ㅣ' 소리가 혀가 펴지고 소리가 얕아서 입을 열기 편하기 때문이다. 또한 사람(ㅣ)이 만물을 여는 데에 참여하고 도와서 통하지 않는 것이 없음을 볼 수 있다.

갈무리 시

음절 소리마다 제각기 가운뎃소리가 있으니
모름지기 가운뎃소리에서 벌림과 오므림을 찾아야

하네.

ㅗ와 ㅏ는 ㆍ에서 나왔으니(양성모음) 합하여 쓸 수 있고
ㅜ와 ㅓ는 ㅡ에서 나왔으니(음성모음) 또한 합하여
쓸 수 있네.

ㅛ와 ㅑ, ㅠ와 ㅕ의 관계는
각각 따르는 곳이 있으니 그 뜻을 미루어 알 수 있네.

ㅣ자의 쓰임새가 가장 많아서
열넷의 소리에 두루 서로 따르네.

4. 종성해(끝소리글자 풀이)

끝소리는 첫소리·가운뎃소리를 이어서 음절을 이룬

다. 이를테면 '즉'자의 끝소리글자는 ㄱ[윽]인데, ㄱ[윽]은 'ㅈ'의 끝에 놓여 '즉'이 되는 것과 같다. '훙'자의 끝소리글자는 ㆁ[웅]인데, ㆁ[웅]은 ㅎ의 끝에 놓여 '훙'이 되는 것과 같다. 혓소리글자, 입술소리글자, 잇소리글자, 목구멍소리글자도 모두 같다.

소리에는 느리고 빠른 차이가 있으니, 평성·상성·거성 음절의 끝소리는 입성 음절 끝소리가 매우 빠른 것과 같은 부류가 아니다. 울림소리 '불청불탁' 글자는 그 소리가 세지 않으므로 끝소리로 쓰면 평성·상성·거성에 마땅하다. 아주 맑은소리 전청, 덜 맑은소리 차청, 아주 흐린소리 전탁 글자는 그 소리가 세므로 끝소리로 쓰면 입성에 마땅하다. 그래서 ㆁㄴㅁㅇㄹㅿ[이니미이리시]의 여섯 글자가 끝소리로 쓰이는 음절은 평성과 상성과 거성이 되고, 나머지 글자가 끝소리로 쓰이는 음절은 모두 입성이 된다.

그렇지만 ㄱㆁㄷㄴㅂㅁㅅㄹ[기이디니비미시리]

의 여덟 글자만으로도 끝소리글자를 적기에 넉넉하다.

이를테면 "**빗곶**(배꽃)"이나 "**영의갗**(여우 가죽)"에서 끝소리글자 '**ㅈ, ㅊ**'을 ㅅ[읏]자로 두루 쓸 수 있어서, '**곳, 갓**'과 같이 오직 ㅅ[읏]자를 쓰는 것과 같다.

또 ㅇ[이]는 소리가 맑고 비어서 반드시 끝소리로 쓰지 않더라도 가운뎃소리만으로 음절을 이룰 수 있다.

ㄷ[디]는 '**볕**'의 끝소리 ㄷ[은]이 되고, ㄴ[니]는 '**군**'의 끝소리 ㄴ[은]이 되고, ㅂ[비]는 '**업**'의 끝소리 ㅂ[읍]이 되며, ㅁ[미]는 '**땀**'의 끝소리 ㅁ[음]이 되고, ㅅ[시]는 토박이말인 '**·옷**'의 끝소리 ㅅ[읏]이 되며, ㄹ[리]는 토박이말인 '**:실**'의 끝소리 ㄹ[을]이 된다.

오음의 느리고 빠름이 또한 각각 스스로 짝이 된다. 이를테면 어금닛소리의 ㆁ[웅]은 ㄱ[윽]과 짝이 되어 ㆁ[웅]을 빨리 발음하면 ㄱ[윽] 음으로 바뀌어 빠르고, ㄱ[윽] 음을 느리게 내면 ㆁ[웅] 음으로 바뀌어 느린 것과 같다. 혓소리의 ㄴ[은] 음과 ㄷ[읃] 음, 입술소리의 ㅁ[음] 음과 ㅂ[읍] 음, 잇소리의 ㅿ[읗] 음과 ㅅ[읏] 음, 목구멍소리의 ㅇ[응] 음과 ㆆ[읗] 음도 그 느리고 빠름이 서로 짝이 되니 이와 같다.

또 반혓소리글자인 ㄹ[을]은 마땅히 토박이말에나 쓸 것이며 한자말에는 쓸 수 없다. 입성의 '彆(별)' 자와 같은 것도 끝소리글자로 마땅히 ㄷ[읃]을 써야 할 것인데 세속 관습으로는 한자말 끝소리를 ㄹ[을] 음으로 읽으니 대개 ㄷ[읃] 음이 바뀌어 가볍게 된 것이다. 만일 ㄹ[을]을 '彆[별]'자의 끝소리글자로 쓴다면 그 소리가 펴지고 늘어져 입성이 되지 못한다.

갈무리 시

맑지도 흐리지도 않은 울림소리를 끝소리에 쓰니

평성, 상성, 거성이 되고 입성은 되지 않네.

아주 맑은소리, 덜 맑은소리, 그리고 아주 흐린소리는
모두 입성이 되어 소리가 매우 빠르네.

첫소리글자를 끝소리글자로 쓰는 이치가 본래 그러한데
다만 여덟 자만 가지고도 쓰임에 막힘은 없네.

오직 ㅇ[이]자가 있어야 마땅한 자리라도
가운뎃소리만으로도 음절을 이루어 또한 통할 수 있네.

만일 '즉'자를 쓰려면 'ㄱ[윽]'을 끝소리로 하고
"훙, 뽇"은 'ㆁ[웅]'과 'ㄷ[읃]'을 끝소리로 하네.

"군, 엽, 땀" 끝소리는 또한 어떨까 하니
"ㄴ[은], ㅂ[읍], ㅁ[음]"을 차례대로 헤아려 보네.

여섯 소리(ㄱㆁㄷㄴㅂㅁ/윽웅은은읍음)는 한자말과 토박이말에 함께 쓰이되
ㅅ[읏]과 ㄹ[을]은 토박이말의 '·옷'과 '실'같이 끝소리로 쓰이네.

오음은 각각 느림과 빠름의 짝을 저절로 이루니
ㄱ[윽] 소리는 ㆁ[웅] 소리를 빠르게 낸 것이네.

ㄷㅂ[은/읍] 소리가 느려지면 ㄴㅁ[은/음]이 되며
ㅿ[웃]과 ㅇ[응]은 그것 또한 ㅅㆆ[읏훙]의 짝이 되네.

ㄹ[을]은 토박이말 끝소리 표기에는 마땅하나 한자말 표기에는 마땅하지 않으니

ㄷ[을] 소리가 가벼워져서 ㄹ[을] 소리가 된 것은 곧 일반 관습이네.

5. 합자해(글자 합치기 풀이)

첫소리·가운뎃소리·끝소리 세 낱글자가 합하여 글자를 이룬다. 첫소리글자는 가운뎃소리글자 위에 쓰기도 하고, 가운뎃소리글자의 왼쪽에 쓰기도 한다. 이를테면 '군'자의 ㄱ[기]는 ㅜ의 위에 쓰고, '엽'자의 ㅇ[이]는 ㅓ의 왼쪽에 쓰는 것과 같다.

가운뎃소리글자는 둥근 것(·)과 가로로 된 것(ㅡ)은 첫소리글자 아래에 쓰니 "· ㅡ ㅗ ㅛ ㅜ ㅠ"가 이것이다. 세로로 된 것은 첫소리글자의 오른쪽에 쓰니 "ㅣ ㅏ ㅑ ㅓ ㅕ"가 이것이다. 이를테면 '튼'자의 ·는 ㅌ[티] 아래에 쓰고, '즉'자의 ㅡ는 ㅈ[지] 아래에 쓰며, '침'자의 ㅣ는 ㅊ[치] 오른쪽에 쓰는 것과 같다. 끝소리글자는 첫소리글자·가운뎃소리글자 아래에 쓴다. 이를테면 '군'자의 ㄴ[은]은 구 아래에 쓰고, '업' 자의 ㅂ[읍]은 어 아래에 쓰는 것과 같다.

첫소리글자에서 서로 다른 두 개의 낱글자 또는 세 개의 낱글자를 나란히 쓰는 '병서'는 이를테면 토박이말의 "ㅼㅏ(땅), ㅽㅏㄱ(외짝), ㅳㅡㅁ(틈)" 따위와 같은 것이다. 같은 낱글자를 나란히 쓰는 각자병서는 이를테면 토박이말에서 "·혀"는 입속의 혀(舌)이지만 "ㆅㅕ" 는 '당겨(引)'를 나타내며, "괴·여"는 '내가 남을 사랑한다(我愛人)'는 뜻이지만 "괴·ㆅㅕ"는 '남에게서 내가 사랑받는다(人愛我)'는 뜻이 되고, "소·다(覆物)"는 '무엇을 뒤집어 쏟다'라는 뜻이지만 "ㅆㅗ·다"는 '무엇을 쏘다(射)'라는 뜻이 되는 따위와 같은 것이다.

가운뎃소리글자를 두 개의 낱글자, 세 개의 낱글자를 합쳐 쓰는 것은 이를테면 토박이말의 "·과[거문고 줄을 받치는 기둥(琴柱)]", "·홰[횃불(炬)]" 따위와 같이 쓰는 것과 같다.

끝소리글자를 두 개의 낱글자, 세 개의 낱글자를 합쳐 쓰는 것은 이를테면 토박이말의 "훍[흙(土)]", "·낛[낚시(釣)], 돐빼[닭때, 유시(酉時)]" 따위와 같이 쓰는 것과 같다. 이들 합용병서는 왼쪽에서 오른쪽으로 쓰며 첫소리글자, 가운뎃소리글자, 끝소리글자 모두 같다.

한자와 언문(한글)을 섞어 쓸 때는 한자음에 따라서 언문의 가운뎃소리글자나 끝소리글자를 보충하는 일이 있으니, 이를테면 '孔子ㅣ魯ㅅ사룸(공자가 노나라 사람)' 따위와 같이 쓰는 것과 같다.

토박이말의 평성·상성·거성·입성의 예를 들면, "활[활(弓)]"은 평성이고 "돌[돌(石)]"은 상성이다.

"·갈[칼(刀)]"은 거성이요, "붇[붓(筆)]"은 입성이 되는 따위와 같다. 무릇 글자의 왼쪽에 한 점을 찍은 것은 거성이고, 두 점을 찍은 것은 상성이며, 점이 없는 것은 평성이다.

　한자말의 입성은 거성과 서로 비슷하다. 토박이말 입성은 한결같지 않아서, 또는 평성과 비슷한 "긷[기둥(柱)], 녑[옆구리(脅)]"과 같은 경우도 있다. 또는 상성과 비슷한 ":낟[곡식(穀)], :깁[비단(繒)]"과 같은 경우도 있다. 또는 거성과 비슷한 "·몯[못(釘)], ·입[입(口)]"과 같은 경우도 있다. 입성에서 점을 찍는 것은 평성·상성·거성의 경우와 같다.

　평성은 편안하고 부드러우니 봄에 해당되어 이는 만물이 편안한 것과 같다. 상성은 부드러움에서 거세져 여름이니, 이는 만물이 점점 무성해지는 것과 같다. 거성은 거세면서도 굳세어 가을이니 만물이 무르익는 것과 같다. 입성은 말소리가 빠르고 막히어 겨울이니 만물이 닫히고 갈무리되는 것과 같다.

　첫소리의 ㆆ[히]와 ㅇ[이]는 서로 비슷해서 토박

이말에서는 두루 쓰일 수 있다.

반혓소리에는 가볍고 무거운 두 소리가 있다. 그러므로 중국 한자음 사전(운서)의 음절 첫소리에서는 오직 하나뿐이며, 또 우리나라 말에서는 비록 가볍고 무거운 것을 구별하지 않더라도 모두 소리를 낼 수 있다. 만약 갖추어 쓰고자 한다면 입술가벼운소리글자(순경음자, ㅸ)의 예에 따라 'ㅇ[이]'를 'ㄹ[리]' 아래 이어 쓰면 반혀가벼운소리글자(반설경음자, ᄛ)가 되니, 혀를 윗잇몸에 살짝 댄다.

• ㅡ가 ㅣ에서 시작되는 소리는 중앙말에 쓰이지 않는다. 아이들 말이나 변두리 시골말에는 드물게 있으니, 마땅히 두 글자를 합하여 나타내려 할 때에는 "ㄱㅣ ㄱㅡ" 따위와 같이 쓴다. 이것은 세로로 먼저 긋고 가로로 나중에 쓰는 것으로 다른 글자와 같지 않다.

갈무리 시

첫소리글자는 가운뎃소리글자의 왼쪽과 위쪽에 쓰는데
'ㆆ[히]'와 'ㅇ[이]'는 토박이말에서는 서로 같이 쓰이네.

가운뎃소리글자 열하나는 첫소리글자에 붙이는데
둥근 것과 가로로 된 것은 첫소리글자 아래에 쓰고
세로로 된 것만 오른쪽에 쓰네.

끝소리글자를 쓰자면 어디에 쓰는가 하니
첫·가운뎃소리글자의 아래에 이어서 붙여 쓰네.

첫·끝소리글자를 각각 합쳐 쓰려면 나란히 쓰고
가운뎃소리글자도 나란히 쓰되 모두 왼쪽부터 쓰네.

토박이말에서는 사성을 어떻게 구별하는가 하니
평성은 '**활**(활)'이요 상성은 ':**돌**(돌)'이네.

'·**갈**(칼)'은 거성이 되고 '**붇**(붓)'은 입성이 되니
이 네 갈래를 보아서 다른 것도 알 수 있네.

소리에 따라 왼쪽의 점으로 사성을 나누니
하나면 거성, 둘이면 상성, 없으면 평성이네.

토박이말 입성은 정함이 없으나 평성·상성·거성처럼 점 찍고
한자말의 입성은 거성과 비슷하네.

우리말은 중국말과 다 다르니
말소리는 있고 글자는 없어 글로 통하기 어려웠네.

하루아침에 신과 같은 솜씨로 정음을 지어 내시니
우리 겨레 오랜 역사의 어둠을 비로소 밝혀 주셨네.

6. 용자례(낱글자 사용 보기)

첫소리글자 ㄱ[기]는 "·감(감), ·골(갈대)"과 같이 쓴다. ㅋ[키]는 "우케(찧지 않은 벼), 콩(콩)"과 같이 쓴다. ㆁ[이]는 "러울(너구리), 서에(성엣장)"와 같이 쓴다.

ㄷ[디]는 "·뒤(띠), ·담(담)"과 같이 쓴다. ㅌ[티]는 "고티(고치), 두텁(두꺼비)"과 같이 쓴다. ㄴ[니]는 "노로(노루), 납(원숭이)"과 같이 쓴다.

ㅂ[비]는 "불(팔), :벌(벌)"과 같이 쓴다. ㅍ[피]는 "파(파), 폴(파리)"과 같이 쓴다. ㅁ[미]는 ":뫼(산), ·마(마)"와 같이 쓴다. ㅸ[비]는 "사·비(새우), 드뷔(뒤웅박)"와 같이 쓴다.

ㅈ[지]는 "**ᅎㅏ**(자), **죠ᅙㅣ**(종이)"와 같이 쓴다. ㅊ[치]는 "**체**(체), **채**(채찍)"와 같이 쓴다. ㅅ[시]는 "**·손**(손), **:셤**(섬)"과 같이 쓴다.

ㅎ[히]는 "**·부헝**(부엉이), **·힘**(힘줄)"과 같이 쓴다. ㅇ[이]는 "**·비육**(병아리), **·ᄇᆞ얌**(뱀)"과 같이 쓴다. ㄹ[리]는 "**·무뤼**(우박), **어름**(얼음)"과 같이 쓴다. ㅿ[ᅀᅵ]는 "**아ᅀᆞ**(아우), **:너ᅀᅵ**(느시)"와 같이 쓴다.

가운뎃소리글자 •는 "**ᄐᆞᆨ**(턱), **·ᄑᆞᆺ**(팥), **ᄃᆞ리**(다리), **·ᄀᆞ래**(가래)"와 같이 쓴다. ㅡ는 "**믈**(물), **발측**(발꿈치), **그력**(기러기), **드레**(두레박)"와 같이 쓴다. ㅣ는 "**·깃**(둥지), **:밀**(밀랍), **피**(피), **·키**(키)"와 같이 쓴다.

ㅗ는 "**논**(논), **톱**(톱), **호·미**(호미), **벼로**(벼루)"와 같이 쓴다. ㅏ는 "**밥**(밥), **낟**(낫), **이아**(잉아), **사·ᄉᆞᆷ**(사슴)"과 같이 쓴다. ㅜ는 "**숫**(숯), **·울**(울타리), **누·에**(누에), **구·리**(구리)"와 같이 쓴다. ㅓ는 "**브ᅀᅥᆸ**(부엌), **:널**(널판), **셔리**(서리), **버들**(버들)"과 같이 쓴다.

ㅛ는 "**쇵**(종, 노비), **·고욤**(고욤), **쇼**(소), **샵툐**(삽주)"와 같이 쓴다. ㅑ는 "**남샹**(남생이), **약**(바다거북), **댜야**(대야), **쟈감**(메밀껍질)"과 같이 쓴다. ㅠ는 "**율믜**(율무), **쥭**(밥주걱), **슈룹**(우산), **쥬련**(수건)"과 같이 쓴다. ㅕ는 "**엿**(엿), **뎔**(절), **벼**(벼), **져비**(제비)"와 같이 쓴다.

끝소리글자 ㄱ[윽]은 "**닥**(닥나무), **독**(독)"과 같이 쓴다. 끝소리글자 ㅇ[웅]은 "**굼벙**(굼벵이), **올창**(올챙이)"과 같이 쓴다. 끝소리글자 ㄷ[읃]은 "**갇**(갓), **싣**(신나무)"과 같이 쓴다. 끝소리글자 ㄴ[은]은 "**·신**(신), **·반되**(반디)"와 같이 쓴다. 끝소리글자 ㅂ[읍]은 "**섭**(섶나무), **굽**(발굽)"과 같이 쓴다. 끝소리글자 ㅁ[음]은 "**범**(범), **:쉼**(샘)"과 같이 쓴다. 끝소리글자 ㅅ[읏]은 "**:잣**(잣), **·못**(연못)"과 같이 쓴다. 끝소리글자 ㄹ[을]은 "**·돌**(달), **별**(별)" 따위와 같이 쓴다.

7. 정인지 서문

천지자연의 소리가 있으면 반드시 천지자연의 문자가 있다. 그러므로 옛사람이 소리를 바탕으로 글자를 만들어서 만물의 뜻을 통하게 하고, 하늘·땅·사람의 세 바탕 이치를 실어서 후세 사람들이 글자를 바꿀 수가 없었다.

그러나 사방의 풍토가 구별되고 말소리의 기운 또한 다르다. 대개 중국 이외의 다른 나라 말은 그 말소리에 맞는 글자가 없다. 그래서 중국 글자를 빌려 쓰고 있는데, 이것은 마치 모난 자루를 둥근 구멍에 끼우는 것과 같으니, 제대로 소통할 때 어찌 막힘이 없겠는가? 중요한 것은 모두 각각 놓인 곳에 따라 자연스럽게 할 것이지, 억지로 같게 해서는 안 될 것이다.

우리 동방의 예악과 문장이 중화(중국)와 같아 견

줄 만하다. 다만 우리말은 중국말과 같지 않다. 그래서 한문으로 된 글을 배우는 이는 그 뜻을 깨닫기가 어려움을 걱정하고, 범죄 사건을 다루는 관리는 자세한 사정을 파악하기가 어려운 것을 근심했다.

옛날 신라의 설총이 이두를 처음 만들어서 관청과 민간에서 지금도 쓰고 있다. 그러나 모두 한자를 빌려 쓰는 것이어서 매끄럽지도 아니하고 막혀서 답답하다. 이두 사용은 오로지 몹시 속되고 일정한 규범이 없을 뿐이니, 실제 언어 사용에서는 그 만분의 일도 소통하지 못한다.

계해년 겨울(1443년 12월)에 우리 임금께서 정음 스물여덟 자를 창제하여, 간략하게 설명한 '예의'를 들어 보여 주시며 그 이름을 '훈민정음'이라 하셨다. 훈민정음은 꼴을 본떠 만들어 글꼴은 옛 '전서체'와 닮았지만, 말소리에 따라 만들어 그 소리는 음률의 일곱 가락에도 들어맞는다. 하늘·땅·사람의 세 바탕

뜻과 음양 기운의 신묘함을 두루 갖추지 않은 것이 없다. 스물여덟 자로 끝없이 바꿀 수 있어, 간결하면서도 요점을 잘 드러내고, 정밀한 뜻을 담으면서도 두루 통할 수 있다.

그러므로 슬기로운 사람은 하루아침이 다 가기도 전에, 슬기롭지 못한 이라도 열흘이면 배울 수 있다. 훈민정음으로 한문을 풀이하면 그 뜻을 알 수 있다. 훈민정음으로 소송 사건을 기록하면, 그 속사정을 이해할 수 있다.

글자 소리로는 맑고 흐린 소리를 구별할 수 있고, 음악 노래로는 노랫가락을 어울리게 할 수 있다. 글을 쓸 때에 글자가 갖추어지지 않은 바가 없으며, 어디서든 뜻을 두루 통하지 못하는 바가 없다. 비록 바람 소리, 두루미 울음소리, 닭 소리, 개 짖는 소리라도 모두 적을 수 있다.

드디어 임금께서 상세한 풀이를 더하여 모든 사

람을 깨우치도록 명하셨다. 이에 신이 집현전 응교 최항과 부교리 박팽년과 신숙주, 수찬 성삼문과 돈녕부 주부 강희안, 행 집현전 부수찬 이개와 이선로 등과 더불어 삼가 여러 가지 풀이와 보기를 지어서, 그것을 간략하게 서술하였다. 바라건대 이 책을 보는 사람은 스승 없이도 스스로 깨치도록 하였다.

그 근원과 정밀한 뜻은 신묘하여 신하 된 자들로서는 감히 밝혀 보일 수 없다. 공손히 생각하옵건대 우리 전하는 하늘이 내리신 성인으로서 지으신 법도와 베푸신 업적이 모든 임금들을 뛰어넘으셨다. 정음 창제는 앞선 사람이 이룩한 것에 따른 것이 아니요, 자연의 이치를 따른 것이다. 참으로 그 지극한 이치가 없는 곳이 없으니, 사람의 힘으로 사사로이 한 것이 아니다. 무릇 동방에 나라가 있은 지가 꽤 오래되었지만, 만물의 뜻을 깨달아 모든 일을 온전하게 이루게 하는 큰 지혜는 오늘을 기다리고 있었

던 것이다.

정통 11년(세종 28년, 1446년) 9월 상순. 자헌대부 예조판서 집현전 대제학 지춘추관사 세자우빈객 정인지는 두 손 모아 머리 숙여 삼가 쓰옵니다.

훈민정음

초판 **1쇄 발행** 2025년 10월 9일

지은이 세종 외 8인(정인지·최항·박팽년·신숙주·성삼문·강희안·이개·이선로)

엮은이 김슬옹 **펴낸이** 정은영 **펴낸곳** 마리북스

ISBN 979-11-93270-42-4 (02710)

Hunminjeongeum

First edition, October 9, 2025
Written by King Sejong and eight others (Jeong Inji, Choe Hang, Bak Paennon, Shin Sukju, Seong Sammun, Gang Huian, Lee Gae, Lee Seonro)
Translated by Jordan Deweger, Kim Suelong | Publisher Jeong Eun-Young | Published Maribooks | ISBN 979-11-93270-42-4 (02710)

all things intact and completes them has led to the long-awaited day for the proclamation of the Jeongeum.

The date of publication of the Hunminjeongeum Haeryebon and the author Jeong Inji

In the beginning of Sejong's 28th year, 1446 AD. Jeong In-ji, Vice Minister of the Court(Jahondaebu), Minister of the Board of Rites, Chief Scholar of the Hall of Worthies, Director of the Office of Annals Compilation, and Right Royal Tutor to the Crown Prince, humbly bows with joined hands and respectfully submits this.

ples, and set them forth in concise form. They were written in such a way that the average person could learn them on their own without an instructor.

A tribute to the greatness of the creator of Hunminjeongeum

The deep origin and precise meaning is mysterious and the subjects cannot presume to reveal it clearly. The courteous consideration of His Royal Highness comes from Heaven so the institutions he created and the contributions he has bestowed have surpassed all other kings. The creation of Jeongeum is not the achievement of anyone who came before, rather it is the principle of nature. In truth, this profound principle is everywhere, it is not the result of a person's private efforts. This country of the East is ancient, however the meaning of all things is generally comprehensible so the great wisdom that keeps

be expressed with these letters, and there is nowhere their meaning cannot be thoroughly communicated. Whether the sound of wind, the cry of the crane, the cluck of the chicken, or the bark of the dog, all sounds can be written down.

Origin of Compilation of Hunminjeongeum Haeryebon

Finally, the King ordered the addition of detailed explanations in order to instruct the people. Thus, together with Choe Hang, Eunggyo(Chief Compiler) of Jiphyeonjeon(the Hall of Worthies); Bak Paengnyeon, Assistant Compiler; Shin Suk-ju; Seong Sammun, Senior Editor; Gang Hui-an, Royal Relations Administrator of Donnyeongbu(Royal Relatives' Office); Lee Gae, Acting Associate Editor of Jiphyeonjeon(the Hall of Worthies); and Lee Seon-ro, I respectfully composed various explanations and exam-

and Humanity, and fully embodies the mysterious harmony of Yin and Yang.

The 28 letters are used in infinite combinations, while simple they express what is vital, while precise they can be easily communicated.

Therefore, wise people can learn it before the morning is over and even those who are not wise can learn it within ten days. When written in these characters one can understand the meaning of the Chinese classics. Moreover, using these characters when dealing with lawsuit cases allows one to understand the real situation.

Phonetic universality of Hunminjeongeum

As for the phonetics of the characters, they can discern clear and thick sounds; and as for music and songs, they perfectly harmonize with the musical pitches. When writing, there is nothing that cannot

borrowed Chinese characters are often awkward, obstructive, and frustrating to use. The use of Idu is extremely coarse and lacks any fixed rules, so it fails to communicate even a ten-thousandth part in actual language use.

History of creation of Hunminjeongeum and excellence of Hunminjeongeum

In the winter of the Year of Gyehae(December 1443), our King created the 28 letters of Jeongeum and provided simple and concise examples and explanations(called 'Yeui'), he named them "Hunminjeongeum(the Correct Sounds for the Instruction of the People)." Hunminjeongeum characters were shaped by imitating forms and their written style emulated ancient seal script; and based on sound, so it fits the seven pitches of Eastern music. It encompasses the fundamental principles of Heaven, Earth,

Chinese characters in order to communicate through writing, this is like trying to put a square handle into a round hole; how can one communicate properly without any problems? The important thing is that all things get along well in their proper place and cannot be forced to be uniform.

Our Eastern land's rites, music, and literature rival those of Huaxia(China). Only our language is different. Therefore, it is difficult to understand the meaning of Chinese classics and the officials who deal with criminal cases have anxiety due to the difficulty of understanding the details of the situation.

Idu history and limitations of using Idu

In ancient times, Seol Chong of Silla first created Idu(method to write Korean through Chinese characters) during the ancient Silla period, which the government and people still use today. But these

7. Preface by Jeong Inji

The value of the sounds and characters of nature

Where there are the sounds of all creation of Heaven and Earth, there must inherently be the characters of all creation. Therefore, the ancients created characters based on sounds, in order to communicate the meanings of all things and to embody the principles of the Three Powers (Heaven, Earth, and Humanity). Thus, people of later generations could not alter these letters.

Diversity of speech sounds and contradiction in borrowing Chinese characters

However, the natural features of all places are different and the spirit of speech sounds are also different. Besides China, other countries do not have letters(writing) that correctly represent their sounds(language). Therefore, these countries borrow

mulberry, /tak/), 독(pot, /tok/)". The final consonant ㅇ /ŋ/ is used as in "굼벙(maggot, /kumpəŋ/), 올챵(tadpole, /ɦoltshʰaŋ/)". The final consonant ㄷ /t/ is used as in "갇(gat, Korean traditional hat, /kat/), 싣(Amur maple tree, /sit/)". The final consonant ㄴ /n/ is used as in "신(shoes, /sin/), 반되(firefly, /pandoj/)". The final consonant ㅂ /p/ is used as in "섭(fire wood, /səp/), 굽(hoof, /kup/)". The final consonant ㅁ /m/ is used as in ":범(tiger, /pəm/), :심(spring of water, /sʌjm/)". The final consonant ㅅ /s/ is used as in ":잣(pine nut, /tsas/), ·못(pond, /mos/)". The final consonant ㄹ /l/ is used as in "돌(moon, /tʌl/), :별(star, /pjəl/)" and so on.

누·에(silkworm, /nuɦəj/), 구·리(copper, /kuɾi/)". ㅓ/ə/ is used as in "브섑(kitchen, /pɨzəp/), :널(plank, /nəl/), 서·리(frost, /səɾi/), 버·들(willow, /pədɨl/)".

- Examples of the use of 'ㅛ/jo/, ㅑ/ja/, ㅠ/ju/, ㅕ/jə/'

ㅛ/jo/ is used as in "죵(servant, /tsjoŋ/), 고욤(lotus persimmon, /koɦjom/), 쇼(cow, /sjo/), 삽됴(Ovate-leaf atractylodes, /saptjo/)". ㅑ/ja/ is used as in "남샹(terrapin, /namsjaŋ/), 약(turtle, /ɦjak/), 다야(washbowl, /taja/), 쟈감(buckwheat husks, /tsjakam/)". ㅠ/ju/ is used as in "율믜(adlay, /ɦjulmɨi/), 쥭(rice spatula, /tsjuk/), 슈룹(umbrella, /sjuɾup/), 쥬련(towel, /tsjuɾjən/)". ㅕ/jə/ is used as in "·엿(taffy, /ɦjəs/), ·뎔(temple, /tjəl/), ·뼈(rice, /pjə/), :져비(barn swallow, /tsjəbi/)".

Examples of the use of the final cosonants

The final consonant ㄱ/k/ is used as in "닥(paper

:녀ㅿ(bustard bird, /nəzi/)".

Examples of the middle vowel letters

• Examples of the use of ' ㆍ, ㅡ, ㅣ'

The middle vowel is used as in "ᆞ톡(chin, /tʰʌk/), ᆞ풋(red bean, /pʰʌs/), 두리(bridge, /tʌɾi/), ᆞ그래(walnut tree, /kʌrai/)". ㅡ /ɨ/ is used as in "믈(water, /mɨl/), ᆞ발ᆞ측(heel, /paltsʰɨk/), 그력(wild goose, /kɨrjək/), 드ᆞ레(well bucket, /tɨɾʌj/)". ㅣ /i/ is used as in "깃(nest, /kis/), :밀(beeswax, /mil/), ᆞ피(millet, /pʰi/), ᆞ키(winnow, /kʰi/)".

• Examples of the use of ' ㅗ/o/, ㅏ/a/, ㅜ/u/, ㅓ/ə/'

ㅗ/o/ is used as in "ᆞ논(rice paddy, /non/), ᆞ톱(saw, /tʰop/), 호ᆞ미(hoe, /homʌj/), 벼ᆞ로(inkstone, /pjəɾo/)". ㅏ /a/ is used as in "ᆞ밥(cooked rice, /pap/), ᆞ낟(sickle, /nat/), 이ᆞ아(heddle(loom part), /ɦiŋa/), 사슴 (deer, /sasʌm/)". ㅜ /u/ is used as in "숫(charcoal, /sus/), 울(fence, /ɦul/),

죠·히(paper, /tsjohʌj/)". ᄎ/tsʰ/ is used as in "체(sieve, /tsʰəj/), 채(whip, /tsʰaj/)". ㅅ/s/ is used as in "·손(hand, /son/), :셤(island, /sjəm/)".

- Examples of the use of guttural sound(laryngeal consonant)

ㅎ/h/ is used as in "·부헝(owl, /puhəŋ/), ·힘(sinew, /him/)". ㅇ/ɦ/ is used as in "·비육(chick, /piɦjuk/), ·부얌(snake, /pʌɦjam/)".

- Examples of the use of semi-lingual sound(lateral consonant)

ㄹ/ɾ, l/ is used as in "·무뤼(hail, /muɾuj/), 어·름(ice, /ɦəɾɨm/)".

- Examples of the use of semi-dental sound(semi-alveolar consonant)

ㅿ /z/ is used as in "아슨(younger brother, /ɦazʌ/),

ㄷ/t/ is used as in "뒤(cogon grass, /tuj/), ·담(wall, /tam/)". ㅌ/tʰ/ is used as in "고·티(cocoon, /kotʰi/), 두텁(toad, /tutʰəp/)". ㄴ/n/ is used as in "노로(roe deer, /noɾo/), 납(monkey, /nap/)".

- Examples of the use of lip sound(labial consonant)

ㅂ/p/ is used as in "볼(arm, /pʌl/), :벌(bee, /pəl/)". ㅍ/pʰ/ is used as in "·파(spring onion, /pʰa/), ·플(fly, /pʰʌl/)". ㅁ/m/ is used as in ":뫼(mountain, /moj/), ·마(yam, /ma/).

- Examples of the use of light lip sound(light labial consonant)

ㅸ/ß/ is used as in "사·비(shrimp, /saßi/), 드·뵈(calabash, /tɨßɨj/)".

- Examples of the use of dental(alveolar) sound

ㅈ/ts/ is used as in "·자(measuring ruler, /tsa/),

One morning, with divine-like ability the King created Jeongeum

Our great nation has been enlightened from the long darkness of our history.

6. Examples of the Use of Letters

Examples of the use of the initial letters

- Examples of the use of the molar sound(velar consonant)

The initial letter ㄱ/k/ is used as in "감(persimmon, /kam/), 갈(reed, /kʌl/)". ㅋ/kʰ/ is used as in "우·케(unhusked rice, /ɦukʰəi/), 콩(bean, /kʰoŋ/)". ㆁ/ŋ/ is used as in "러울(raccoon, /rəŋul), 서·에(floating ice, /səŋəj/)".

- Examples of the use of lingual sound(alveolar consonant)

(brush)' becomes the checked tone
Looking at these four types one can understand other things as well.

To distinguish between sounds, dots on the left divide the four tones
One means the high tone, two means the rising tone, and none means the even tone.

The checked tone of native Korean is not determined so like the even, rising, and high tones dots are added
The checked tone of Sino-korean words is similar to the high tone.

Our language is completely different from Chinese
If there are sounds but no letters for them, it is difficult to communicate in writing.

to its right.

Where does one write the final consonant letters?
They are attached below the initial consonant letters and middle vowel letters.

If the initial and final consonant letters are respectively combined and written then they are written side by side
The middle vowel letters are also all written side by side from the left.

How are the four tones distinguished in native Korean?
The even tone is '활/hwal/'(arrow) and the rising tone is ':돌/tol/'(stone).

'·갈/kal/'(knife) becomes the high tone and '·붇/put/

outlying villages, and when they are properly combined and expressed they are written together as "ㄱㅣ /kjʌ/, ㄱㅣ /kjɨ/". This is different from other letters since vertical strokes must be written first and horizontal strokes are written second.

Summarizing verse for explanation of combining letters

Initial consonant letters are written above and to the left of middle vowel letters

'ㆆ /ʔ/' and 'ㅇ /ɦ/' are used interchangeably in native Korean.

The eleven middle vowel letters are attached to the initial consonant letters

The middle vowels with a round dot(·) or a horizontal stroke(ㅡ) are written below the initial consonant, while those with a vertical strokes are written

Writing the semi-lingual sound

The semi-lingual sound(lateral consonant) contains both light and heavy sounds. Therfore in the Chinese rhyme dictionaries, each syllable has only one initial sound; yet in our language, even without distinguishing between light and heavy sounds, all can still be pronounced. If one wants to distinguish between them, following the example of a light labial sound letter(ㅸ), if 'ㅇ/ɦ/' is written consecutively under letter(ㄹ) then it becomes a light semi-lingual sound(ᄛ), as the tongue lightly touches the upper teeth ridge.

Writing method of combining ㅣ and ·, ㅣ and ㅡ vertically

Sounds beginning with ㅣ/i/ from ·/ʌ/ and ㅡ/ɨ/ are not used in the standard language. However, they do occur rarely in children's language or the dialects of

tone is the same as in the case of even tone, rising tone, and high tone.

Comparison of tone characteristics in the four seasons

The even tone is calm and soft so it corresponds to Spring like the tranquility of all things in harmony. The rising tone grows stronger from gentleness so it corresponds to Summer as all things gradually become thick and dense. The high tone is forceful and firm so it corresponds to Autumn as all things become ripen and mature. The checked tone is fast and constricted so it corresponds to Winter as all things are closed and storing away of all things.

The initial sounds ㆆ /ʔ/ and ㅇ /ɦ/

The initial sounds ㆆ /ʔ/ and ㅇ/ɦ/ are similar so they can be used interchangeably in native Korean.

checked) can be seen through the examples of "활(arrow, /hwal/)" as the even tones, 돌(stone, /tol/) as the rising tone, "·갈(knife, /kal/)" as the high tone, and "·붇(brush, /put/)" as the checked tone.

Writing dots the left for tones

As a general rule, one dot placed to the left of a letter indicates a high tone, two dots indicate a rising tone, and no dots indicate an even tone.

The checked tone

The checked tone of Sino-korean words is similar to the high tone. The checked tone of native Korean is not fixed so it can become similar to the even tone as in "긷(pillar, /kit/), 녑(flank, /njəp/)". Or similar to the rising tone as in ":낟(grain, /nat/), :깁(silk /kip/)". Or similar to the high tone as in "·몯(nailn /mot/), '입(mouth, /ɦip/)". The use of dots in the checked

Chicken, 5-7pm, /tʌrks-pstaj/)".

Writing the letters laterally attached

These combined letters are written from left to right, and the same principle applies to initial, medial, and final letters alike.

A notation that mixes Chinese characters and native Korean characters

When Chinese characters and Eonmun(Hanguel, native Korean script) are mixed the sounds of the Chinese characters are followed by the addition of the middle or final sounds of Eeomun, for example '孔子ㅣ/i/ 魯ㅅ/s/ :사룸(Confucius is a person of "Lu", /sarʌm/)' and so on.

Tone of the native word

The four tones of native Korean(even, rising, high, and

rean "혀/hjə/" means tongue while "혀/xjə/" means pull, "괴여/koj-ɦjə/" means 'I love another' but "괴여/koj-ɦ'jə/" means 'I am loved by another,' and "소다/so-da/" means to pour something but also "쏘다/s'o-da/" means to shoot something, and so on.

Writing the middle vowel letters laterally attached

The combination and use of two or three middle vowels can be seen in the example of the native Korean word "과/kwa/" which means the bridge of a Korean harp, and "홰/hwaj/" which means torch.

Writing the final consonant letters laterally attached

The combination and use of two or three final consonants in one character can be seen in the examples of native Korean words such as "훍(흙, earth/dirt, /hʌlk/)", "낛(fishing, /naks/)", and "돐빼(the hour of the

written below ㅌ/tʰ/, ㅡ/ɨ/ of the character '즉/tsɨk/' is also written below ㅈ/ts/, and l/i/ of the character '침/tsʰim/' is written to the right of ㅊ/tsʰ/.

The position of the final consonant letter

Final consonants are written below the initial and middle sounds. For example, in the character of '군/kun/', ㄴ/n/ is written below 구/ku/, and for the character '업/ŋəp/', ㅂ/p/ is written below 어/ŋə/.

Writing the initial consonant letters laterally attached

In the initial letters two or three different letters can be combined and written side by side, as in the examples of the native Korean words "짜(the earth /sta/), 짝(an odd member of a pair, /ptsak/), and 씀(gap, /pskɨm/)." The same letters can be combined and written side by side. For example, in native Ko-

5. Explanation of Combining Letters

The structure of the syllable and writing

The initial, middle, and final letters are combined to make syllables. The initial consonant letter may be written either above the medial vowel letter or to its left. For example, in the character '군/kun/,' ㄱ/k/ is written above ㅜ/u/ and for the character '업/ŋəp/,' ㅇ/ŋ/ is written to the left of ㅓ/ə/.

The position of the initial consonant letter by the properties of the middle vowel letter

As for the medial vowel letters, those with a round dot(ㆍ/ʌ/) and a horizontal line(ㅡ/ɨ/) are written below the initial consonant, those are "ㆍ/ʌ/ ㅡ/ɨ/ ㅗ/o/ ㅛ/jo/ ㅜ/u/ ㅠ/ju/." The vertical vowels ㅣ/i/ ㅏ/a/ ㅑ/ja/ ㅓ/ə/ ㅕ/jə/ are written to the right of the initial consonants. For example, in the 'ᄐᆞᆫ/tʰʌn/', ㆍ/ʌ/ is

native Korean.

The five sound classes each naturally form pairs of slowness and quickness
The sound of ㄱ /k/ is the quicker pronunciation of ㆁ /ŋ/.

The sounds of ㄷ /t/ ㅂ /p/ become ㄴ /n/ ㅁ /m/ when pronounced slowly
ㅿ /z/ and ㅇ /ɦ/, as well as ㅅ /s/ and ㆆ /ʔ/ are counterparts.

As for ㄹ /l/, it is the appropriate mark for a final sound of native Korean but not for sino–korean words
ㄷ /t/ is pronounced lightly to become ㄹ /l/, which has become simply a matter of common custom.

ㅇ/ɦ/ is the only one that can be omitted in a position where final would normally be required
Only using middle sounds one can form syllables without final sound.

If one writes the character "즉/tsɨk/" then ㄱ/k/ is used as the final sound
ㆁ/ŋ/ and ㄷ/t/ are used as the final sounds for "홍/xoŋ/, 볃/pjət/".

What are the final sounds of "군/kun/, 업/ŋəp/, 땀/t'am/"?
They are "ㄴ/n/, ㅂ/p/, ㅁ/m/" respectively.

The six sounds(ㄱ/k/ ㆁ/ŋ/ ㄷ/t/ ㄴ/n/ ㅂ/p/ ㅁ/m/) can be used for both Sino-Korean words and native Korean
ㅅ/s/ and ㄹ/l/ are used as the final sounds for only like '옷/os/'(clothes) and '실/sil/'(thread) for only in

be a checked tone.

Summarizing verse for explanation of the final sounds

When sonorant consonants, which are neither clear nor thick, are used as finals
The syllable belongs to the even, rising, or high tones, but not to the checked tones.

Completely clear, slightly less clear, and completely thick sounds
Are all checked tones, so the pronunciation is extremely quick.

The principle of using initial letters again as finals is by nature the same
And just eight letters are sufficient without any obstruction in usage.

same way, the lingual sounds(alveolar consonants) of ㄴ/n/ and ㄷ/t/, the labial sounds of ㅁ/m/ and ㅂ/p/, the dental(alveolar) sounds of ㅿ/z/ and ㅅ/s/, and the guttural sounds ㅇ/ɦ/ and ㆆ/ʔ/ also correspond as pairs of slow and fast articulations.

Usage of semi-lingual ㄹ/l/

Semi-lingual(lateral consonant) letter ㄹ/l/ is appropriately used for native Korean words but not for Sino-Korean words. The character "彆(볃, /byeot/)" should properly use the final consonant ㄷ/t/ in accordance with the checked tone(ip-seong), but in common usage, the final sound of Chinese characters has come to be pronounced with ㄹ/l/, thus, the original ㄷ/t/ sound has been softened and lightened through popular convention. If ㄹ/l/ is used as the final sound of the character ':별(彆, /pjəl/)' then the sound is smoother and extended so it can no longer

final sound the middle sound itself can still form a syllable.

The final sound of '볃/pjət/' is ㄷ/t/, the final sound of '군/kun/' is ㄴ/n/, the final sound of '업/ŋəp/' is ㅂ/p/, the final sound of '땀/t'am/' is ㅁ/m/, ㅅ/s/ is the final sound of the native Korean '·옷/os/'(clothes), and ㄹ/l/ is the final sound of the native Korean ':실/sil/'(thread).

The quickness and slowness of the final consonant letter

The slowness and quickness of the five sound classes(velar, alveolar, labial, dental, and glottal) also naturally pair with one another. For example, among the molar sounds(velar sounds) ㆁ/ŋ/ with ㄱ/k/ becomes a complement so when ㆁ/ŋ/ is pronounced quickly it changes to ㄱ/k/ which is pronounced forcefully, and when ㄱ/k/ is pronounced slowly it changes to ㆁ/ŋ/ and becomes more relaxed. In the

completely clear, semi-clear, completely thick sounds have a strong sound so when used as a final sound they rightly become checked tones. Accordingly, whose final sound is one of the six letters ㆁ/ŋ/ ㄴ/n/ ㅁ/m/ ㅇ/ɦ/ ㄹ/l/ ㅿ/z/ become even, rising, or high tones, whereas syllables whose final sound is any of the other letters all become checked tones.

Using only 8 final consonant letters as every final consonants

However the eight letters ㄱ/k/ ㆁ/ŋ/ ㄷ/t/ ㄴ/n/ ㅂ/p/ ㅁ/m/ ㅅ/s/ ㄹ/l/ alone are sufficient for writing final consonants. For example, in "빗곶 (Pear blossom, /pʌjskots/)" and "엿의갗(Fox pelt, /ɦjəzɦɨkas/)" the final consonants 'ㅈ' and 'ㅊ' can all be written as 'ㅅ,' so it is the same as using only 'ㅅ' as the final consonant, as in "곳"/kos/ and "갓"/kas/. The sound of ㅇ/ɦ/ is clear and empty so even if it is not used as a

is the same as ㄱ/k/ is placed at the end of ㅈ/tsɨ/, becoming '즉'/tsɨk/. The final sound of the character '뽕'/xoŋ/ is ㅇ/ŋ/, which is the same as ㅇ/ŋ/ is placed at the end of ㅗ/xo/, becoming '뽕'/xoŋ/. The same goes with the lingual sound(alveolar consonant) letter, the labial sound letter, the dental sound(alveolar consonant) letter, and the guttural sound letter.

Properties of the final consonant letter and tone connection

There are differences between slow and fast sounds, so the final sounds of the even, rising, and high tones are not of the same as the final sounds of the checked tone, which are extremely fast. The sonorant letters, which are neither clear nor thick, have sounds that are not strong; therefore, when used as final sounds, they are suitable for the even tone, the rising tone, and the high tone. The letters with

Yin quality like ㅡ/ɨ/, can also be combined and used together.

The relation of ㅛ/jo/ and ㅑ/ja/ and ㅠ/ju/ and ㅕ/jə/
Each has something they follow, so one can thereby realize their meaning.

The letter ㅣ/i/ is most widely used
So it accompanies the 14 vowel sounds.

4. Explanation of the Final Sounds

Meaning of the final consonant letter and examples

The final sounds along with the initial and middle sounds form syllabic characters. For example, the final sound of the character '즉'/tsɨk/ is ㄱ/k/, which

letters formed when the double medial vowels are combined with ㅣ/i/, namely: "ㅛㅐ/waj/ ㅠㅔ/ ㅛㅐ/jojaj/ ㅠㅖ/jujəj/".

ㅣ/i/ can combine with both deep and shallow, closed and open sounds because the tongue flattens and the sound is light, making it easy to open the mouth. Moreover, one can see that human beings ㅣ/i/ also take part in opening all things and assist so that nothing remains unconnected.

Summarizing verse for explanation of the middle sounds
For every syllabic sound there is a middle sound
Openness and closedness must be found in the middle sounds.

Since ㅗ/o/ and ㅏ/a/ are medial vowels of Yang quality, like ·/ʌ/, they can be combined and used together
Likewise, ㅜ/u/ and ㅓ/ə/, being medial vowels of

same principle.

Writing laterally attached the middle vowel letters

When two medial letters are combined, such as ㅗ/o/ and ㅏ/a/, since they are both positive(Yang) medial vowels like ㆍ/ʌ/, they combine to form ㅘ/wa/. ㅛ/jo/ and ㅑ/ja/ come from ㅣ/i/, so they combine to form ㅛㅑ/joja/. Since both ㅜ/u/ and ㅓ/ə/ are negative(Yin) medial vowels like ㅡ/ɨ/, when combined, they form ㅝ/wə/. ㅠ/ju/ and ㅕ/jə/ also come from ㅣ/i/, so they combine to form ㅠㅕ/jujə/. Being of the same kind, these sounds belong to the same group, and thus they can combine without discord.

The middle vowel letter, combining with 'ㅣ'

The ten medial vowels "ㅓ/ʌj/ ㅢ/ɨj/ ㅚ/oj/ ㅐ/aj/ ㅟ/uj/ ㅔ/əj/ ㅛ/joj/ ㅒ/jaj/ ㆌ/juj/ ㅖ/jəj/" are formed by combining basic vowel with ㅣ/i/. There are four medial

From them all kinds of sounds are generated.

3. Explanation of the Middle Sounds

Function of the middle vowel letter and example

The medial sound(vowel) resides in the middle of the syllable and, by combining with the initial and the final, forms a syllable. The middle sound of the letter '툰'/tʰʌn/ is • /ʌ/ and since • /ʌ/ is placed between ㅌ/tʰ/ and ㄴ/n/, the syllable becomes '툰'/tʰʌn/. The middle sound of '즉' /tsɨk/ is ㅡ /ɨ/, so when ㅡ /ɨ/ is placed between ㅈ /ts/ and ㄱ /k/ it becomes '즉/tsɨk/'. The middle sound of the letter '침'/tsʰim/ is ㅣ/i/, which is the same as ㅣ/i/ between ㅊ/tsʰ/ and ㅁ/m/ becomes '침'/tsʰim/. "ㅗ/o/ ㅏ/a/ ㅜ/u/ ㅓ/ə/ ㅛ/jo/ ㅑ/ja/ ㅠ/ju/ ㅕ/jə/" of "홍/xoŋ/ 땀/t'am/ 군/kun/ 엽/ŋəp/ 욕/jok/ 샹/zjaŋ/ 슐/sjut/ 볃/pjət/" all follow this

Summarizing verse for explanation of Initial sounds

The sounds of "ㄱ/k/ ㅋ/kʰ/ ㄲ/k'/ ㆁ/ŋ/" are the molar sound(velar consonant) letters

The lingual sound(alveolar consonant) letters are "ㄷ/t/ ㅌ/tʰ/" and "ㄸ/t'/ ㄴ/n/".

"ㅂ/p/ ㅍ/pʰ/ ㅃ/p'/ ㅁ/m/" are namely the labial sounds

Of the dental(alveolar) sound letters there are "ㅈ/ts/ ㅊ/tsʰ/ ㅉ/ts'/ ㅅ/s/ ㅆ/s'/".

"ㆆ/ʔ/ ㅎ/h/ ㆅ/x/ ㅇ/ɦ/" are namely the guttural sounds(laryngeal consonants)

ㄹ/ɾ/ is a semi-lingual, ㅿ/z/ is semi-dental(alveolar).

The twenty-three letters serve as the consonant letters for the initial sounds

Since speech sounds originate from it, it is called "mother(mo)."

In regards to the molar sound(velar consonant), ㄱ/k/ is the initial sound of the letter '군'/kun/, so ㄱ/k/ and ㅜㄴ/un/ join to become '군'/kun/. The initial sound of the letter '쾌'/kʰwaj/ is ㅋ/kʰ/, so ㅋ/kʰ/ and ㅙ/waj/ join to become 쾌/kʰwaj/. The initial sound of the letter '뀨'/k'ju/ is ㄲ/k'/, so ㄲ/k'/ and ㅠ/ju/ join to become the letter '뀨'/k'ju/. ㅇ/ŋ/ is the initial sound of '업'/ŋəp/, which is the same as ㅇ/ŋ/ and ㅓㅂ/əp/ join to become '업'/ŋəp/.

The lingual sound(alveolar consonant) letters "ㄷ/t/ ㅌ/tʰ/ ㄸ/t'/ ㄴ/n/", the labial sound letters "ㅂ/p/ ㅍ/pʰ/ ㅃ/p'/ ㅁ/m/", the dental sound letters "ㅈ/ts/ ㅊ/tsʰ/ ㅉ/ts'/ ㅅ/s/ ㅆ/s'/" and the guttural sound letters "ㆆ/ʔ/ ㅎ/h/ ㆅ/x/ ㅇ/ɦ/" as well as the semi-lingual and the semi dental(alveolar) sound letters "ㄹ/ɾ/ ㅿ/z/" all have the same principle.

Jeongeum only has 28 letters
Yet as one studies their deepness and complexity they can uncover the depth of their origin.

The meaning is profound yet the language is accessible so the common people can be taught easily
This is bestowed by Heaven - how could it ever have been accomplished through human wisdom and artifice?

2. Explanation of Initial Sounds

Meaning of the initial consonant letter and examples

The initial sounds of Jeongeum correspond to the initial consonants(shengmu, the mother-sounds) of a syllable as defined in Chinese rhyme dictionaries.

As the final sound is compared with Earth, it means the motionlessness of Yin
The sound of the letter ceases here and so is fixed.

The completion of a syllable depends on the use of the middle sound,
And through this, humans are able to assist in harmonizing Heaven and Earth.

The function of Yang connects through Yin
When it reaches its utmost and extends, it then turns back and returns.

Though initial consonant characters and final consonant characters are distinguished as Heaven and Earth,
One can understand the principle of using initial consonant characters for final consonant positions.

When the middle vowel calls, the initial sound responds
That Heaven comes before Earth is the principle of nature.

The thing that answers becomes both the initial and the final sound
Just as all things are born from the Earth and ultimately return to it.

Yin turns into Yang, and Yang turns into Yin
One movement and one stillness become the root of each other.

As initial sounds have the meaning of renewal
And with the movement of Yang, it becomes the master of Heaven.

As •/ʌ/ is found in all 8 letters
Only the action of Heaven universally flows to all places.

There is also a reason why the sounds(ㅛ/jo ㅑ/ja ㅠ/ju
ㅕ/jə/) incorporate the human sound(ㅣ/i/)
Among all beings that participate in Heaven and Earth, humans are the most divine.

Also, if one observes the profound principle of the three sounds(initial, middle and final)
Hardness and softness, as well as Yin and Yang are naturally present.

The middle vowels according to the action of Heaven, are divided into Yin and Yang
While the initial sounds, as the merits of Earth, represent hardness and softness.

ㅏ/a/ also comes from Heaven(•/ʌ/) so it is already opened wide
It springs forth in things and affairs and is brought to completion in humans.

The single round dot means original birth
It comes from Heaven, becomes Yang, and is placed above or outside.

As ㅛ/jo/ ㅑ/ja/ unites ㅣ/i/, they become another again
One can see this meaning in the shape of the two round dots.

As ㅜ/u/ and ㅓ/ə/ and ㅠ/ju/ and ㅕ/jə/ come from Earth
As can be understood from the examples, why then explain something that is naturally understood?

Their deep meaning cannot be inferred easily yet.

・/ʌ/ is modeled after heaven and the sound is the deepest
Its round form is like a bullet.

ㅡ/ɨ/ is neither deep nor shallow
Its flat shape is modeled after the Earth.

ㅣ/i/ is modeled after a standing person and its sound is light
Herein are embodied the three fundamental principles of Heaven, Earth, and Human.

ㅗ/o/ comes from Heaven(・/ʌ/) so it is almost closed
Its shape follows modeled after the roundness of Heaven combined with the flatness of Earth.

As " ㄲ/k'/ ㄸ/t'/ ㅃ/p'/" are completely thick sounds
So too are " ㅉ/ts'/ ㅆ/s'/" and " ㆅ/x/".

If completely clear letters are written side by side
they become completely thick letters(tense letters)
However, 'ㆅ/x/' alone is derived from 'ㅎ/h/' and
does not follow this rule.

As for "ㅇ/ŋ/ ㄴ/n/ ㅁ/m/ ㅇ/ɦ/" and "ㄹ/ɾ/ ㅿ/z/"
Their sound is neither clear nor thick.

If ㅇ/ɦ/ is written underneath a labial sound it becomes a light labial sound
As the guttural sound(laryngeal consonant) becomes stronger and the lips close lightly.

There are 11 middle vowels and they are also modeled after their form

It is Earth as one of the Five Elements, late summer as one of the seasons and "Gung" as one of the sounds on the Eastern pentatonic scale.

The sounds of speech are naturally both clear and thick
The important thing is when the first sound comes out they must be carefully observed and considered.

As "ㄱ/k/ ㄷ/t/ ㅂ/p/" are completely clear sounds
So too the sounds of "ㅈ/ts/ ㅅ/s/ ㆆ/ʔ/" are completely clear sounds.

The similar thing for "ㅋ/kʰ/ ㅌ/tʰ/ ㅍ/pʰ/ ㅊ/tsʰ/ ㅎ/h/" is that
Of the five sounds each one is a slightly less clear sound(aspirated sound).

The guttural sound(laryngeal consonant) is Water as one of the Five Elements, winter as a season, and "U" as one of the sounds on the Eastern pentatonic scale
The molar sound(velar consonant) is Tree as one of the Five Elements, spring as a season, and "Gak" as one of the sounds on the Eastern pentatonic scale.

The lingual sound(alveolar consonant) is "Chi" as one of the sounds on the Eastern pentatonic scale, summer as a season and Fire as one of the Five Elements
The dental sound(alveolar consonant) is "Sang" as one of the sounds on the Eastern pentatonic scale, winter as a season and Metal as one of the Five Elements.

While the labial sound originally does not have a determined direction or number

Once the meaning of these five letters is understood, the principles of sound are naturally revealed.

There are also semi-lingual(semi-alveolar) sound(ㄹ) and the semi-dental(semi-alveolar) sound(ㅿ) letters
The imitations are similar but their structure is seemingly different.

The sounds of "ㄴ/n/ ㅁ/m/ ㅅ/s/ ㅇ/ɦ/" are not strong
Even though final in order, they are first when forming characters.

As the four seasons and the force of Heaven and Earth meet
There is nothing that does not harmonize with the Five Elements and Five-tone scale(pentatonic scale).

teeth, and throat

From here seventeen initial sound letters come.

The molar sound(velar consonant) character follows the appearance of the back of the tongue blocking the throat

Only ㆁ/ŋ/ and ㅇ/ɦ/ are similar but assume different meanings.

The lingual sound(alveolar consonant) character follows the shape of the tongue touching the upper teeth ridge

The labial sound character assumed the shape of the mouth.

The dental sound(alveolar consonant) character and the guttural sound(laryngeal consonant) follows the shape of the dental and throat

Summarizing verse for explanation of the designs of the letters

The harmony of Heaven and Earth is originally the spirit of one, thus
Yin-Yang and the Five Elements mutually become the beginning and the end.

All things between Heaven and Earth have form and sound
Yet their origin is not two, but unified through principle and number.

In creating the Jeongeum letters, they were chiefly modeled on forms
Following the intensity of the sound one more stroke is added.

The sounds come from the molars, tongue, mouth,

The single fundamental spirit flows universally and endlessly; the four seasons are in an endless cycle, just as the end of all things is again the start of all things, spring comes again from winter. In the same way, initial consonants again become final consonants and final consonants again become first consonants.

Admiration of Hunminjeongeum's principles and praise for King Sejong the Great, who created Hunminjeongeum

Ah! With the creation of the Jeongeum(Correct Sounds), the principles of all things in Heaven and Earth, have been fully encompassed, so this Jeongeum(the Correct Sounds) is truely marvelous. Surely, it was Heaven that awakened the mind of King Sejong the Great and, through his hands, brought forth the creation of Jeongeum.

ment and prospering, thus they are the work of Heaven. The final consonants hold the meaning of fixation and stillness and thus they are the work of Earth. As for the middle vowels, they follow the emergence of the initial consonants and the completion of the final consonants, thus combined, they are the work of humans.

The middle vowels are the most important since they join the initial consonants and final consonants to form syllables. Likewise, all things are born of and built upon Heaven and Earth but making them useful and mutually beneficial depends entirely on humans.

As for the use of initial letters again as final consonants, Yang is dynamic so it is Heaven, Yin is static so it is also Heaven, and Heaven, though in reality is actually divided between Yin and Yang it presides and governs over all things.

all things return to the Earth.

Meaning of the combining writing the Initial consonant letter, middle vowel letter, final consonant letter

Like the combination of initial, middle and final letters to form a syllable, motion and stillness become mutual roots with the meaning of Yin and Yang which are mutually transforming. That which moves is Heaven, and that which is still is Earth. It is humans who contain both movement and stillness. Generally, the Five Elements are the movement of the cosmos in Heaven, the fulfillment of substance on Earth, and for humans they are benevolence, courtesy, sincerity, righteousness, and wisdom as the movement of the cosmos and the liver, heart, spleen, lung and kidney as the fulfillment of substances.

The initial consonants hold the meanings of move-

initial consonants are the way of the Earth. If one of the middle vowels is deep then the other is shallow, if one is pursed then the other is open, as this follows the division of Yin and Yang and the provision of the force of the Five Elements is the function of Heaven. Among the initial sounds, some are hollow(guttural), some are blocked(velar), some are flying(lingual), some are caught(dental), some are heavy(labial-heavy), and some are light(labial-light). Thus firmness and softness are revealed, and here the foundation of the Five Elements is established—this is the merit of Earth.

As middle vowels are either deep or shallow, and either rounded or open, they are pronounced first and as the Five Sounds of the initial consonants, being either clear or thick, follow in response, becoming both the initial and final consonants. This is indicated from how all things are born from the Earth and

and the place from which Earth comes. ㅡ/ɨ/ corresponds to the number 10 of the earth at which Earth is made complete. Only the vowel 'ㅣ/i/' has neither a fixed position nor elemental number, for the human being is the embodiment of the truth of Mugeuk(the limitless), where the energies of Yin, Yang, and the Five Elements subtly mingle and fuse, making it truly impossible to define any fixed placement or enumeration.

Accordingly the middle sounds naturally contain Yin and Yang, the Five Elements and directional numbers.

Comparing the middle vowel letter and the initial consonant letter

Let's compare initial consonants and middle vowels. The Yin and Yang of the middle vowels are the way of Heaven. And the hardness and softness of the

it is the place that gives birth to Fire. Next, ㅓ/ə/ originated; the number of Earth is 4 and it is the place that gives birth to Metal. ㅛ/jo/ second originated form Heaven; the number of Heaven is 7 at which Fire is made complete. Next, ㅑ/ja/ originated; the number of Heaven is 9 at which Metal is made complete. ㅠ/ju/ second originated from Earth; the number of Earth is 6 at which Water is made complete. Next, ㅕ/jə/ originated; the number of Earth is 8 at which Tree is made complete.

Because Water(ㅗ/o/ ㅠ/ju/) and Fire(ㅜ/u/ ㅛ/jo/) cannot be separated from the spirit and are at the interacting origin of Yin and Yang, we need to purse the lips when pronouncing them. Because Tree(ㅏ/a/ ㅕ/jə/) and Metal(ㅓ/ə/ ㅑ/ja/) are firmly fixed on the foundation of Yin and Yang, we need to open the mouth unrounding the lips.

·/ʌ/ corresponds to the number 5 of the heaven

lord over all things are capable of participating with Yin and Yang.

Numbering properties of the middle vowel letter and the Yin-Yang and Five-Elements

Because these letters are created from the forms of Heaven(·), Earth(ㅡ) and Humans(ㅣ), they contain the principle of the Three fundamental Elements. Therefore, just as the Three fundamental Elements are the source of all things, and Heaven is first among the Three Elements, ·/ʌ/ ㅡ/ɨ/ ㅣ/i/ are the head of the eight letters, with ·/ʌ/ as first among the three.

ㅗ/o/ first originated from Heaven; the number of Heaven is 1, and it is the place that gives birth to water. Next, ㅏ/a/ originated; the number of Heaven is 3 and it is the place that gives birth to Tree. ㅜ/u/ first originated from Earth; the number of Earth is 2 and

nounced by starting with ㅣ/i/.

ㅗ/o/ ㅏ/a/ ㅜ/u/ ㅓ/ə/ originate from Heaven and Earth and are thus primary letters(The first-generated letters). ㅛ/jo/ ㅑ/ja/ ㅠ/ju/ ㅕ/jə/ begin with ㅣ/i/, which symbolizes to human, making them secondary letters(The re-generated letters). ㅗ/o/ ㅏ/a/ ㅜ/u/ ㅓ/ə/ have one dot, meaning they were created first and are the primary letters(The first-generated characters). ㅛ/jo/ ㅑ/ja/ ㅠ/ju/ ㅕ/jə/ have two dots, meaning they were created second and are secondary letters.

The dots of ㅗ/o/ ㅏ/a/ ㅛ/jo/ ㅑ/ja/ are on the upper side or outside, meaning they come from Heaven and are equated with Yang. The dots of ㅜ/u/ ㅓ/ə/ ㅠ/ju/ ㅕ/jə/ are on the bottom or inside, meaning they come from Earth and are equated with Yin.

·/ʌ/ is part of all eight letters just as Yang leads Yin and flows through all things. ㅛ/jo/ ㅑ/ja/ ㅠ/ju/ ㅕ/jə/ are all combined through humans(ㅣ), who being

ered, its shape is formed by joining ㅡ/ɨ/ and ·/ʌ/ which also represents the first interaction of Heaven and Earth.

ㅓ/ə/ is the same middle vowel(negative vowel) as ㅡ/ɨ/, but pronounced with the mouth opend wider, the shape is formed by joining ·/ʌ/ and ㅣ/i/ which again means that all things begin with Heaven and Earth, but wait upon humans for their completion.

Properties of primary vowel letters(monophthongs) and secondary vowel letters(diphthongs)

ㅛ/jo/ is the same middle vowel(positive vowel) as ㅗ/o/, but is pronounced by starting with ㅣ/i/. ㅑ/ja/ is the same middle vowel(positive vowel) as ㅏ/a/, but is pronounced by starting with ㅣ/i/. ㅠ/ju/ is the same middle vowel(negative vowel) as ㅜ/u/, but is pronounced by starting with ㅣ/i/. ㅕ/jə/ is the same middle vowel(negative vowel) as ㅓ/ə/, but is pro-

of the character resembles a human standing upright.

The following eight medial vowels are pronounced, some with the lips puckered(rounded) and others with the lips spread open.

ㅗ/o/ is the same middle vowel(positive vowel) as ㆍ/ʌ/, but pronounced with the lips more puckered, the reason why the shape of ㆍ/ʌ/ and ㅡ/ɨ/ are combined, because the shape resembles Heaven and Earth as they first interact.

ㅏ/a/ is the same middle vowel(positive vowel) as ㆍ/ʌ/, but is pronounced with the mouth opend wider, the reason why the shape is formed by joining ㅣ/i/ and ㆍ/ʌ/, meaning that all things come from Heaven and Earth, but wait upon humans for their completion.

ㅜ/u/ is the same middle vowel(negative vowel) as ㅡ/ɨ/, but is pronounced with the lips more puck-

sonant) it becomes softer. This is because the guttural sound(laryngeal consonant) is strong so the lips are momentarily closed.

Properties of the 17 middle vowel letters phoneme and the Yin-Yang and Five-Elements

As for middle vowel letters, there are eleven letters.

・/ʌ/ is pronounced by contracting the tongue, thus the sound becomes deep, like when Heaven opens at the hour of the Rat(11pm-1am). he round shape of the character was modeled after Heaven.

ㅡ/ɨ/ is pronounced by slightly contracting the tongue, thus it is neither deep nor shallow, like when the earth opens at the hour of the Ox(1am-3am). The flat from of the character was modeled after Earth. As for 'ㅣ/i/', the tongue is not contracted so the sound is light, like when humans are born during the hour of the Tiger(3am-5am). The vertical shape

water.

Since ㄱ/k/ is based on the substance of a Tree, ㅋ/kʰ/ is like a tree which has flourished and grown dense, and ㄲ/k′/ is like a Tree that has fully matured and grown strong. All of these letters are formed according to the shape of the molars.

When completely clear letters are written side by side they become completely thick, meaning that the completely clear sounds become completely thick when coalesced. However, for partially clear letters, only the guttural sounds(laryngeal consonants) become completely thick, this is because the sound of ㆆ/ʔ/ is too deep and cannot coalesce, whereas the sound of ㅎ/h/ is lighter and thus coalesces and becomes a completely thick sound.

Properties of the labial sound

When ㅇ/ɦ/ is written below a lip sound(labial con-

"ㄴ/n/ ㅁ/m/ ㅇ/ɦ/" are the least strong of the sounds and even though they are at the back of the order but they come first when forming letters. ㅅ/s/ and ㅈ/ts/ are completely clear but ㅅ/s/ is less strong compared to ㅈ/ts/ and thus comes first when forming letters.

In regards to the molar sound(velar consonant) ㆁ/ŋ/, the back of the tongue blocks the throat so sound is produced through the nose, but the ㆁ/ŋ/ sound and the ㅇ/ɦ/ sound are similar so the Rhyming Dictionary often confuse the two sounds. ㆁ/ŋ/ is designed after the shape of the throat so it is not used for the beginning of molar sounds(velar consonant) letters.

The throat correlates to Water and the molar teeth correlate to Tree, ㆁ/ŋ/ is a molar sound(velar consonant) that is similar to ㅇ/ɦ/, just as tree sprouts which grow from water are soft and remain full of

lars, therefore they correspond to the directions of the North and the East. The tongue and teeth are next, therefore they correspond to the directions of the South and the West. The lips are situated at the end. Earth does not have any fixed direction but it contributes to the flourishing of the four seasons. Thus, each initial consonant has its own directional number and corresponds to the Five Elements and Yin Yang.

Classification and properties from the perspective of sound quality of the initial consonant letter

Also, let's say about sounds as clarity and thickness. "ㄱ/k/ ㄷ/t/ ㅂ/p/ ㅈ/ts/ ㅅ/s/ ㆆ/ʔ/" are completely clear, whereas "ㅋ/kʰ/ ㅌ/tʰ/ ㅍ/pʰ/ ㅊ/tsʰ/ ㅎ/h/" are partially clear. And "ㄲ/k'/ ㄸ/t'/ ㅃ/p'/ ㅉ/ts'/ ㅆ/s'/ ㆅ/h'/" are extremely thick. "ㆁ/ŋ/ ㄴ/n/ ㅁ/m/ ㅇ/ɦ/ ㄹ/ɾ/ ㅿ/z/" are neither clear nor thick.

The lips are square and joined, and are regarded as Earth as one of the Five Elements. The lip sound(labial consonant) is full and broad just as the Earth is, which contains all things. As a season it is late summer, and is the note of "Gung" on the Eastern pentatonic scale.

The directional mapping of speech sounds in Five Elements theory

Water is the source from which all things are generated, and fire is the function through which all things are completed; therefore, among the Five Elements, water and fire are the greatest.

The throat is the gate from which all sounds come and the tongue is the organ which distinguishes sounds thus, the guttural and lingual sounds(alveolar consonant) are the most important among the five sounds.

The throat is the furthest back, followed by the mo-

pentatonic scale.

Molars are long and uneven, and are thus recognized as Tree among the Five Elements. The molar sound(velar consonant) is similar to the guttural sound(laryngeal consonant) but is fuller and has form, like a tree which arises from water. As a season it is spring, and is the note of 'Gak' on the Eastern pentatonic scale.

The tongue moves quickly and is thus regarded as Fire among the Five Elements. The sound of the tongue rolls and flies like a fire blazes and flares up. As a season it is summer, and is the note of "Chi" on the Eastern pentatonic scale.

Teeth are strong and edged, and are regarded as Metal as one of the Five Elements. The dental sound(alveolar consonant) is high and compressed just as metal is crushed and remade. As a season it is fall, and is the note of "Sang" on the Eastern pentatonic scale.

The semi-lingual sound(semi-alveolar consonant) letter ㄹ/r/ and the semi-dental sound(semi-alveolar consonant) letter △/z/ are made to resemble the shape of the tongue and tooth respectively, so the meaning of adding one stroke does not apply because it follows a different system of forming characters than the above system.

The Five Elements theory of speech sounds

Generally speaking the human speech sounds are based on the Five Elements(Water, Fire, Earth, Metal, Tree). Therefore, they are in accordance with the four seasons and the Eastern pentatonic scale.

The throat is deep and moist, thus as one of the Five Elements it is regarded as Water. Just as water is clear and flows freely, the sound that comes from the throat is free and unhindered. As one of the seasons it is winter, and is the note of "U" on the Eastern

are 17 initial consonant letters. The molar sound(velar consonant) letter ㄱ/k/ resembles the blocking of the throat with the back of the tongue. The lingual sound(alveolar consonant) letter ㄴ/n/ resembles the tongue touching the upper gums(teeth-ridge). The lip sound(labial consonant) letter ㅁ/m/ resembles the shape of the mouth. The dental sound(alveolar consonant) letter ㅅ/s/ resembles the shape a tooth. The guttural sound(laryngeal consonant) letter ㅇ/ɦ/ resembles the shape of the throat.

The sound of ㅋ/kʰ/ is more strongly pronounced than ㄱ/k/ so one more stroke is added to the character. According to this system ㄷ/t/ comes from ㄴ/n/, ㅌ/tʰ/ from ㄷ/t/, ㅂ/p/ from ㅁ/m/, ㅍ/pʰ/ from ㅂ/p/, ㅈ/ts/ from ㅅ/s/, ㅊ/tsʰ/ from ㅈ/ts/, ㆆ/ʔ/ from ㅇ/ɦ/ and ㅎ/h/ from ㆆ/ʔ/, as a stroke is added to signify stronger pronunciation, with the exception of ㆁ/ŋ/.

In between Gon(☷, Terra, Symbol of femininity) and Bok(☷, Return, Symbol of new growth) there is the Great Absolute, and motion and stillness are followed by the formation of Yin and Yang. Out of all the living things, what can exist without Yin and Yang? Accordingly, the speech sounds of humans are also governed by Yin and Yang, though people do not take careful notice of this. The creation of this Jeongeum("Correct Sounds") has not arisen from a difficult task requiring wisdom, rather it is simply the result of persistent research of the principle of the speech sounds. The principle is not two, but one; thus, it must be used by both spirits of Heaven and of Earth.

Creating principle of 17 initial consonant letters

All of the 28 letters of Hunminjeongeum are each created by imitating their respective shapes. There

Part 2.
Explanation and Examples of the "The Correct Sounds for the Instruction of the People"

1. Explanation of the Designs of the Letters

The way of Heaven, Earth and the principle of the speech sounds

The principle of Heaven, Earth, and all things is only one, that of the interacting principles of Yin(陰, shadow) and Yang(陽, light) and the Five Elements.

nant letters.

Writing the middle vowel attached

"•/ʌ/ —/ɨ/ ㅗ/o/ ㅜ/u/ ㅛ/jo/ ㅠ/ju/" are attached below initial consonant letters.

"ㅣ/i/ ㅏ/a/ ㅓ/ə/ ㅑ/ja/ ㅕ/jə/" are written to the right of initial consonant letters.

Combining to form syllables

In general, individual letters must always be combined to form syllables.

Drawing a dot on the left indication tone

One dot on the left of the character indicates a high tone, two dots indicate a rising tone, and no dots indicate an even tone. As for the checked tone(Ipseong, a quickly ending tone), the dots have the same meaning, but the pronunciation is faster.

(穰)'/zjaŋ/.

ㅠ/ju/ is like the middle sound of the character '슏(戌)'/sjut/.

ㅕ/jə/ is like the middle sound of the character '볃(彆)'/pjət/.

Writing the final consonant letter

The final consonant letters are the same as those used for the initial consonant letters.

Writing the light labial sound

If ㅇ/ɦ/ is written immediately after a lip sound(labial consonant), it becomes a light lip sound(light labial consonant, ㅱ).

Writing the consonant characters laterally attached

If initial consonant letters are combined, they are written side by side, the same goes for final conso-

The middle vowel letter font and pronunciation

ㆍ/ʌ/ is like the middle sound of the character '둔(呑)'/tʰʌn/.

ㅡ/ɨ/ is like the middle sound of the character '즉(即)'/tsɨk/.

ㅣ/i/ is like the middle sound of the character '침(侵)'/tsʰim/.

ㅗ/o/ is like the middle sound of the character 퐁(洪)'/xoŋ/.

ㅏ/a/ is like the middle sound of the character '땀(覃)'/tʼam/.

ㅜ/u/ is like the middle sound of the character '군(君)'/kun/.

ㅓ/ə/ is like the middle sound of the character '업(業)'/ŋəp/.

ㅛ/jo/ is like the middle sound of the character '욕(欲)'/ɦjok/.

ㅑ/ja/ is like the middle sound of the character '샹

of the character 'ᅏ(慈)'/ts'ʌ/.

ㅊ/tsʰ/ is a dental sound(alveolar consonant), like the first sound of the character '침(侵)'/tsʰim/.

ㅅ/s/ is a dental sound(alveolar consonant), like the first sound of the character '슏(戌)'/sjut/.

ㆆ/ʔ/ is a guttural sound(laryngeal consonant), like the first sound of the character '흡(挹)'/ʔɨp/.

ㅎ/h/ is a guttural sound(laryngeal consonant), like the first sound of the character '허(虛)'/hə/.
When written consecutively it is like the first sound in the character 薭(洪)'/xoŋ/.

ㅇ/ɦ/ is a guttural sound(laryngeal consonant), like the first sound of the character '욕(欲)'/ɦjok/.

ㄹ/ɾ/ is a semi-lingual sound(lateral consonant), like the first sound of the character '려(閭)'/ɾjə/.

ㅿ/z/ is a semi-teeth(semi-alveolar consonant), like the first sound of the character '샹(穰)'/zjaŋ/.

first sound of the character '두(斗)'/tu/.

When written consecutively it is like the first sound of the character '땀(覃)'/t'am/.

ㅌ/tʰ/ is a lingual sound(alveolar consonant), like the first sound of the character '튼(呑)'/tʰʌn/.

ㄴ/n/ is a lingual sound(alveolar consonant), like the first sound of the character '나(那)'/na/.

ㅂ/p/ is a lip sound(labial consonant), like the first sound of the character '볃(彆)'/pjət/.

When written consecutively it is like the first sound of the character '뽀(步)'/p'o/.

ㅍ/pʰ/ is a lip sound(labial consonant), like the first sound of the character '표(漂)'/pʰjo/.

ㅁ/m/ is a lip sound(labial consonant), like the first sound of the character '미(彌)'/mi/.

ㅈ/ts/ is a dental sound(alveolar consonant), like the first sound of the character '즉(即)'/tsɨk/.

When written consecutively it is like the first sound

twenty-eight new letters, no more than to make it convenient for all people to easily learn and use them in their daily lives.

2. Definition and Examples of the Basic Consonants and Vowels

The initial consonant letter font and pronunciation

ㄱ/k/ is a molar sound(velar consonant), like the first sound of the character '군(君)'/kun/.

When written consecutively it is like the first sound of the character '끆(虯)'/k′ju/.

ㅋ/kʰ/ is a molar sound(velar consonant), like the first sound of the character '괘(快)'/kʰwaj/.

ㆁ/ŋ/ is a molar sound(velar consonant), like the first sound of the character '업(業)'/ŋəp/.

ㄷ/t/ is a lingual sound(alveolar consonant), like the

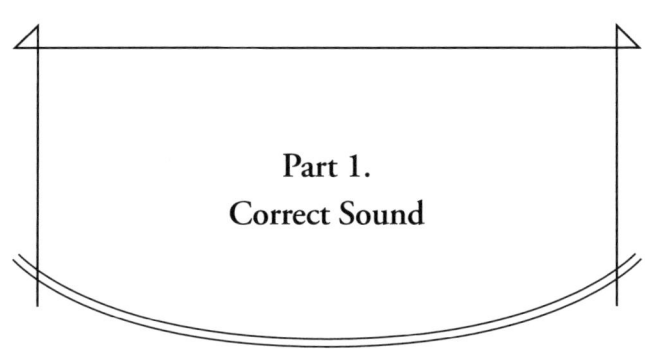

Part 1.
Correct Sound

1. Preface by King Sejong

The speech of our country is different from Chinese and as a result does not coordinate well with written Chinese characters. Therefore, even if the common people who cannot read or write have something to say, there are many people who are unable to express it in writing. Finding this pitiful, I have created the native alphabet for everyday use.

King Sejong's purpose in promulgating Hunminjeongeum was clear: everyone should be able to freely express and share their feelings and thoughts using an easy writing system. We hope this small book will convey the spirit behind the creation of Hunminjeongeum to readers everywhere and help them understand how this writing system brought light to our people's long darkness.

We are deeply grateful to Mr. Jordan Deweger for his clear and accurate English translation, and to Professor Jeong Pil-jeong for carefully reviewing the English translation.

On Hangeul Day, 2025
Kim Seul-ong

read together. This is why we have published it as a pocket book that you can carry with you and read anytime, anywhere. We have complied both Korean and English editions with the hope of sharing the value of Hunminjeongeum, created and promulgated by King Sejong, with readers both at home and abroad.

The Haerye book of Hunminjeongeum contains the purpose of the creation of Hangeul, letter design principles, commentaries on usage, etymological meanings, as well as various sample sentences. The introductory preface, written by King Sejong himself, illustrates the spirit of self-reliance to devise a new, befitting system for the Korean language due to the incompatibility of Chinese characters and Korean language, King Sejong's love towards people who were illiterate in Chinese to help them communicate freely and easily with a simple writing system, and the spirit of practicality for all people to readily learn

Preface to the Pocket Edition of Hunminjeongeum Haerye: Modern Korean and English

On the 579th Hangeul Day, KBS broadcast a special program titled "Prosper! Naratmalssam"(Korean Language, directed by Lee Gwang-rok). Every moment of the program was moving, but one scene left a particularly deep impression: diverse participants, including foreigners, reading the Hunminjeongeum Haerye(hereafter, Haerye) together.

The Haerye is a classic among classics that all Koreans—indeed, all people around the world—should

Correct Sounds for the Instruction of the People

Hunminjeongeum

Written by King Sejong et al 8

Translated by Jordan Deweger·Kim Seul-ong